Laugh

Rinse

Repeat

Humorous Bite-Size Stories from the "Other Side" of the Dental Chair

Terry Hans

RDH

Laugh Rinse Repeat

Humorous Bite-Size Stories from the "Other Side" of the Dental Chair

Copyright © 2023 by Terry Hans, RDH
(Registered Dental Hygienist)

ISBN: **9798853628830**

Disclaimer:

Laugh, Rinse, Repeat is a work of fiction. It reflects the author's present recollections of experiences over time. Any similarities of medical conditions, patient names or office location of an actual patient are entirely coincidental. All names and characteristics have been changed. Places and time have been rearranged to suit the convenience of the book. Some passages have been embellished, and often two or three separate instances have been combined into one narrative to provide a greater impact.

DEDICATION

My husband Butch
My daughters Tracey and Christy
My sons-in-law Lance and Paul
My grandsons Jacob, Zachary, Kyle and Austin

Thank you for encouraging my writing journey.

Acknowledgments

I'm fortunate to have had a long-term employment history in a handful of practices I worked in over the years. As a familiar face, patients were able to get to know me and feel comfortable telling me just about anything. Sometimes, it was definitely too much information. Compiling these stories has been the culmination of forty-five years of a dental hygiene career.

I owe a huge thank you to the dentists who employed me and always kept humor in the workplace. In each office, the dentist created an environment of a family, helping us to work together more effectively.

I thank my co-workers, who are treasured friends, and always had my back. They encouraged me and helped me recall many of these memories.

I thank my patients for sharing their lives and inspiring so many stories.

I am indebted to Mary Concannon for her insistence, urging me to write down these stories.

I greatly appreciate Diana Kane, my sister, and fellow dental hygienist, for her dental expertise, encouragement, and convincing me to write this book.

I am grateful to the talented, award-winning authors in NC Scribes and Light of Carolina Christian Writers for mentoring me, listening to these stories, and giving great feedback, week after week.

I want to give a special shout-out and expressions of heartfelt gratitude to Nancy Panko, Ellen Edwards Kennedy, Linda Loegel Hemby, Emmy Bittler, and Cathy Zachary for their assistance in editing and arranging the story order.

The support and encouragement from my family, in the years it took for this book to become a reality, will never be forgotten. Without them, this book would never have been completed.

I thank God for guidance in pursuit of my dreams in connection with my writing journey.

Introduction

The Great Wig Caper

In 1967 I chose my profession in an unorthodox manner. After scanning the college catalog, I registered for the only curriculum that didn't require additional math classes. I didn't have a clue what I would be doing. In my neighborhood, you went to the dentist only when you had a toothache. Dental Hygienist was a foreign word to me.

On the first day of orientation, I had a rude awakening. Yes, I was in college, or so I thought. Hippie attire was the rage, but the Dental Hygiene curriculum had a stringent set of specific regulations. While other students on campus wore tie-dye shirts and frayed ripped jeans, I had to wear skirts. The restrictions filled an entire manual exclusive to this department. The most intrusive directive, not mentioned until orientation, was that hair must be in a pixie cut. Absolutely no exceptions were permitted.

On the first day of classes, I discovered many students with long hair had dropped out of the program. Some got those short ugly haircuts, but others, like me, were more resourceful and purchased cheaply-made short wigs. The teachers balked. Evidently, no other class was as brazen. However, nowhere in the handbook could they find a ruling banning wigs; therefore, they grudgingly accepted our hairpieces.

The courses were demanding and proved to be grueling. Initially, my extent of a dental term was "tooth." Now I had to learn the names and numbers of teeth and their dental anatomy. Intense study sessions with classmates Sherrie, Ginny, and Judy crammed in all the information we needed to learn before clinic time. Without their support, I would never have completed the program.

The clinic sessions started with a set of plaster teeth clamped to a workbench with a rubber band for the cheeks. Their elasticity allowed ample stretching with little resistance. However, I was unprepared for how difficult mouth access would become when a patient with facial muscles, a tongue, and tender gums was in my treatment chair.

When I had my classmate in the dental chair for the first time, I hardly knew how to hold an instrument or use it correctly. We were each other's guinea pigs. It was only fair for my patient to clean my teeth after I butchered her gums. I remember we bled a lot and went home with very sore mouths. Good thing we knew about salt water rinses to soothe the tissue.

Nearing the end of our senior year, we took a big gamble. Our instructors were always serious, so we became masters of making our own fun to relieve our stress. On the last day of clinic, about twenty of us switched wigs. The redhead was now a blonde, our brunette had perky locks of silver, and I had a jet-black wig covering my auburn hair. We looked ridiculous, and the clinic was in utter chaos!

Finally, we calmed our giggles before class began and got to work. The instructors didn't notice until they came to check our patients, clipboard in hand. After doing a double take at each assigned workstation, our most feared, stern-faced professor had trouble controlling her amusement. Holding her hand up as if to say "no more," my examiner turned away to collect herself. Her shoulders shook in laughter. I guess they were human, after all.

After forty-five years, I retired from dental hygiene. The profession I knew nothing about in the beginning brought me great satisfaction and personal accomplishments. Employers, co-workers, and patients have encouraged me to share my experiences.

What I have to show for the exhausting school schedule, back-breaking days of standing cleaning teeth, wrists aching, fingers bitten, and reassuring patients who hate having their teeth cleaned is a collection of stories based on true events. Some passages have been embellished, and often two or three separate instances have been combined into one narrative to provide a greater impact. Names have been changed to avoid embarrassment, but these hilarious anecdotes are too precious not to share.

I hope you will have as much fun reading them as I did writing them.

You just can't make this stuff up!

Enjoy!

Terry Hans

PART ONE
The Early Years
Buffalo, New York
1967-1980

1.   My Hallmark Moment
2.   Caged
3.   Money-Money Everywhere
4.   House of Walters
5.   Papal Pilgrimage
6.   Wham-O
7.   Liberty Bell Blues
8.   Bumper Carts
9.   A Bleary-Eyed Whimsical Vision
10. Murdering the Monarch
11. A Stone Cold Mystery
12. Sparkling Celebration
13. The Landlord's Surprise
14. Breaking Tradition
15. The Imperfect-Perfect Wedding
16. Polka Dots-Oh My

PART TWO
Rochester, New York
1980-2005

17. Frozen in Time
18. Diet Guru
19. Secret Admirer
20. Embrace the Present
21. A Permanent Solution
22. Bucking Bronco
23. An Arrested Development
24. Hooking the Big One
25. What in the World is a Key Fob?
26. Disappearing Car Caper
27. Miracle on the St. Lawrence River
28. Hitting the Waves
29. Queen's Wave
30. Moulin Rouge
31. Fancy Pants in France
32. Lost Luggage Fiasco
33. Stuck Again
34. Slip Sliding Away
35. Nut or Lug Nut
36. Showtime
37. Critter Hill
38. Reality TV
39. Swinging Pineapple
40. Michelin Man
41. Thumbs Up
42. The Fickle Finger of Fate
43. Don't Fool with the Master

PART THREE
Rochester, New York
1991-2005
(Years overlap-working in two offices)

44.   Opportunity Comes Knocking

45.   Building a Friendship

46.   Hole-y Drywall

47.   White Coat Syndrome

48.   Unexpected Lockup

49.   Strange Cravings

50.   Novice Chef

51.   Sweet Tooth

52.   Unusual Art Gallery

53.   Prizefighter

54.   Out of the Mouth of Babes

55.   Petting Zoo Caper

56.   Bearing it All

57.   Barnyard Dentistry

58.   Holiday Treats

59.   Things That Go Boom in the Night

60.   Ghostly Encounter

61.   Things Are Not Always as They Seem

62.   Concrete Adventure

63.   Runaway Walker

64.   Technology to the Rescue

65.   Grannie Bloomers

66.   Godiva Night

PART FOUR
Southern Connection
2005-2012

67. Our Crazy Cat Lady
68. Decoration Day
69. Am I Gone?
70. Speedway at the Biltmore
71. The Implant Debacle
72. Wild Kingdom Bunco
73. Smokin' Hot
74. An Innocent Gardner
75. A Southern Belle's Exhumation

PART ONE

The Early Years

Buffalo, New York

1967-1980

1

My Hallmark Moment

Our dad grew up in the Great Depression with non-existent dental care. Since both my sister and I chose careers in dental hygiene, we constantly had Dad in a dental chair cleaning his remaining teeth and trying to teach him better oral hygiene.

My sister Dee and our dad lived in Buffalo, NY, while I lived in Rochester, about 80 miles away. Our employers were alumni of the same dental school. These dentists had served in the military and wanted to give back to Dad, who was a highly decorated WWII veteran. Dad traveled back and forth between cities, and the two dentists restored his mouth free of charge.

One day while Dad was with my sister, she phoned me, "Dad's teeth are starting to take shape, but there are a few that are beyond saving."

Dee made the appointments and coordinated a plan between our two employers. I felt so bad that Dad was losing teeth, one by one. He was fretting about losing two molars.

"Dad, they'll make you great-looking partials, and you'll be all set," I reassured him.

He looked at me with sad eyes. "Honey, I have been trying so hard to take care of my teeth."

Dad's comment gave me an idea. He would be at my sister's for the extractions. As a grandmother of four little boys, who are constantly losing teeth, I knew Hallmark had a card for just that occasion; I'd purchased four in the past. It had an adorable green alligator with a string tied to a tooth. The cheery caption read, "You're losing a tooth. Don't be sad."

My hunt began. After checking three Hallmark stores, I was about to give up. I decided to try one more place. As I entered, I asked, "Do you have the card with the alligator on it for losing a tooth?"

With the sales lady's assistance, I hit the jackpot. Triumphantly, she held the card and exclaimed, "I don't believe I've ever seen this one. It's so cute."

We chatted, and when I got to the register, I told her I had purchased this card before, so I knew it existed. She and her co-worker were talking with each other as I was leaving the store. Just as I got to the door, the sales lady shouted out, "By the way, how old is the little darling?"

Oh, I couldn't resist! I was grinning from ear to ear. Then, without any hesitation or explanation, I simply answered as I walked out the door, "Oh, he's eighty-four!"

2

Caged

It was 1970, and I was a recently-graduated dental hygienist, anxious to start my new job. However, my excitement faded as I realized I had chosen a profession that made me feel like a white-coated villain in a world where most people dread dental visits. Nevertheless, I became determined to make this work and to give my patients a pleasant experience. Engaging people in conversation about themselves was my way of making them forget why they were there.

Charlie was a former patient who had relocated to New Hampshire. He came in for a dental visit while he was in town, and I extended my sympathy. "It must have been hard coming home for your father's funeral."

"Thank you," he said. "This trip almost got me arrested."

"I can't imagine how traveling in Buffalo could get you arrested."

"The story is so outlandish I can hardly believe it myself," he laughed. "You probably remember that my father was a veterinarian. My father's colleague reached out to me in desperate need of additional equipment for the shelter he founded. I was happy to donate whatever I could."

Charlie continued, "I loaded the extra equipment into my father's station wagon. My two young daughters begged to come with me for this last trip to the veterinary clinic. They are such animal lovers; I thought showing them where Papa's things were going would be fun."

I commented, "I bet they loved it."

"Yes, they were excited. The clinic was just across the bridge into Canada, and they wanted to see Niagara Falls."

"That's one of my favorite places," I bubbled.

"In most cases, crossing the border is a relatively easy process. Customs agents merely asked where you were born, and you were on your way." Charlie continued, "Since equipment filled the cargo space to the brim, I made the girls comfortable in the back seat with lots of pillows and blankets. It had been an exhausting week, and I had a lot to accomplish before we returned home. I was relieved the girls were being quiet."

"I'm sure settling your dad's estate is a monumental task," I added sympathetically.

Charlie said, "It sure is! As I approached the front of the line to go through customs, unbeknownst to me, the agents were on the alert for my vehicle. Numerous phone calls came over the newly implemented 911 line alerting a possibly dangerous situation, a possible kidnapping."

Charlie smiled and said, "When the customs agent quizzed me about what was in the back cargo compartment, I shrugged my shoulders. Finally, I answered, I don't need this paraphernalia, and I'm just dumping..." Charlie crossed the border four times that week with no problems until now. "What seems to be the problem, officer? I am just getting rid of this stuff."

"Mister, that is the wrong answer!" The annoyed customs agent remarked.

I looked at Charlie with wide-eyed anticipation.

"Exit the vehicle," the agent commanded.

Not allowing Charlie to continue, the officer grabbed his radio, and immediately three more customs agents appeared, surrounding the vehicle. Charlie was hoping his daughters had fallen asleep. He said, "Not until I stepped out of the car did I realize what was causing the commotion."

Cuddled up, looking comfy, his daughters were fast asleep. The only problem was that they had crawled into the dog cages in the back of the station wagon. "It's no wonder I was getting a lot of attention."

"My mischievous daughters climbed out of the cages, barking and pretending they were puppies. It took a lot of explaining, but after the girl's performance, the customs agent believed my bizarre story. Boy, was I relieved! Can you believe I almost caused an international incident?" Charlie chuckled.

Laughingly, I said, "Charlie, that's a great story, and your girls are old enough to always remember the day Daddy almost got himself arrested."

3

Money-Money-Everywhere

Getting Nellie to relax in the dental chair was challenging, however I did my best. Engaging her in conversation was the perfect distraction. She loved telling me about her newly-married daughter, Frances, and we began discussing the events of her shopping trip last Friday. She referred to it as the day they almost needed a bail bondsman.

Nellie said she and Frances patiently waited at the bank's drive-up window. Engrossed in conversation, they paid little attention to the vehicle ahead. But, when they noticed the occupant put a package marked with large black lettering into the open mechanical drawer, they were curious.

Frances commented, "That old bashed-up SUV looks like Uncle Jack's."

"Yeah, it does, but Jack lives over a hundred miles away." Nellie quickly dismissed the idea.

From the passenger seat, Frances could see the teller shoving wads of loose bills into the drawer, still wide open to the outside. Suddenly, Frances gasped as a green cloud of money exploded into the air as the wind carried currency from the extended drawer.

"Oh, my gosh!" Nellie cried out, "That poor man is losing his money."

Nellie told me, "Bills flew everywhere, reminding me of a game show where money swirled around in a glass enclosure while the contestant tried to pluck currency from the air. As we were fretting about the money blowing away, the driver managed to grab some of the cash and sped off."

"What in the world?" Frances exclaimed.

Clueless that something was wrong, they pulled forward to the drive-up teller. Nellie and Frances were frantic, trying to explain to the teller about the airborne money.

The bank employee was screaming and backing away from the window. Then, with panicked gestures, she attempted to wave us off and shouted, "Get out, there's a bomb!"

Trying to process the scene, Nellie just waited her turn.

The teller yelled, "Lady, the bank was robbed, and there's a bomb!"

Finally, it sunk in as they saw everyone running out of the bank. Nellie stepped on the gas, and they peeled out of the parking lot as sirens were shrieking and numerous police cars arrived on the scene.

"Mom, are you okay?" Frances shouted above the sirens.

They looked at each other, shaken, but the duo just continued on their way to run other errands, unaware that they should have stayed at the bank. Little did they know the police were looking for them since they fled the hold-up scene and were potential suspects. Moreover, bank security cameras had captured the "junker" and Nellie's car behind it. Police reasoned that it would be an impossible coincidence that the two vehicles weren't connected in the robbery.

It never occurred to Nellie or Frances to go back to the bank. About thirty minutes later, they had an epiphany. Realizing they had witnessed the entire robbery, their eyewitness account could assist in apprehending the robbers.

The mother and daughter returned to find police everywhere and the area roped off with crime scene tape. When they noticed the bomb-squad vehicle, and a robot carrying a package the size of a brick, they pulled into an adjoining parking lot.

Officers surrounded the car, telling the women to put their hands in the air and exit slowly. Believing Nellie and Frances were accomplices, the police officers were about to handcuff them and seat them in a squad car for transport to the station house.

At that moment, police radios squawked that the get-away car was reported as stolen and dumped about a mile from the bank. The ancient vehicle had broken down. The robber had to flee on foot and was apprehended.

Overhearing the police transmission, Frances whispered, "Mom, that was Uncle Jack's car. What are the odds of cars belonging to brother and sister being in line at the bank at the exact time when the robbery was in progress? No wonder they thought we were involved."

Everyone was relieved to learn the package was not a bomb. Nellie and Frances gave their statements and were allowed to get back in their car.

The six-o'clock news lead report was about the bomb threat at the bank. Mother and daughter were relieved the footage shown was of the abandoned car and the suspect in custody, not them sitting in the line at the bank.

Nellie laughed. "Do you know that is the fourth time Jack's car has gone missing?"

They both giggled, and Frances said, "That bank robber should have stolen a better car!"

I saw the news story and had many questions, but I knew I would never get Nellie's teeth cleaned, so I saved those inquiries for her next visit.

4

The House of Walters

Let me introduce you to a very colorful character named Barbara. She is a delightful woman and became one of my favorite patients. I had the pleasure of meeting Barbara and her husband, Walter, soon after graduating from dental hygiene school. They were among my first patients at Dr. O'Dell's. We instantly connected when we realized my husband had gone to school with her son, Walter.

Barbara always had an interesting anecdote to share. At today's appointment, she had us rolling in laughter as she shared pictures from New Year's Eve. Persuaded by his mom, her soon-to-be-married son would frolic as Baby New Year at the church's annual *Sweep Out the Old, Ring in the New Party*. Unfortunately, Maria, the bride-to-be, was not privy to this information.

The two Walters excused themselves just before midnight, and Maria feared they would miss the big moment. Standing alone, Maria looked around, confused, wondering what had happened to her fiancé.

Precisely, at the stroke of midnight, the crowd sang the melancholy *Auld Lang Syne* as everyone shared hugs and kisses. Watching from the sidelines, Maria felt lonely and neglected but smiled as she saw Barbara's husband, Walter, shuffling onto the stage, dressed as Father Time. He played the role perfectly, hunched over with a long white beard and cane.

Following Father Time was the missing fiancé, Barbara's son, Walter. As Baby New Year paraded around the crowd celebrating the beginning of the new decade, the laughter drowned out the young woman's gasp. Maria turned crimson as she watched her Walter clad only in a makeshift diaper, top hat, and a sash across his bare chest welcome in 1970. "What kind of crazy family am I marrying into?" she wondered.

A few months after Barbara's appointment, I was delighted to receive an invitation to her son's upcoming nuptials. It was difficult not to notice that the bride's father's name was also Walter. I thought *the irony of three Walters. How confusing*!

My husband and I attended their beautiful wedding ceremony and reception. A handsome man in a tux approached me. He leaned over to introduce himself, saying, "Sorry we haven't met, but I'm the bride's brother; my name is (you guessed it) Walter."

"Oh, my gosh," I exclaimed. "Did I hear you correctly? Are you another Walter? Oh, umm, pleased to meet you, Walter."

I walked away, trying not to be noticed as I chuckled, but I couldn't wait to find my husband. I told him, "No one will ever believe this at work. What are the odds of all four men being named Walter? That's a hoot!"

After attending their wedding, we became good friends with Walter and Maria. Quite often, Maria had to explain the Walters. It was always attention-grabbing to hear Maria simplify, reciting the spiel she had down pat. "I know it's hard to believe, but my husband's name is Walter, his father's name is Walter, my father's name is Walter, and to complete the insanity, my brother's name is Walter."

Maria's speech always brought smiles to the unsuspecting listener. Furthermore, guests invited to the House of Walters could relax because they never had to worry about forgetting someone's name. Walter always did the trick!

5

Papal Pilgrimage

Barbara practically skipped into our office for her dental appointment. It was surprising since she was a sixty-five-year-old woman who had just graduated from a walker after knee surgery. At her last appointment, Barbara told us she would travel with her church delegation on their pilgrimage to Toronto to see the Pope. As I saw her cheerful mood, I thought *no one likes to see the dentist that much; she must have quite a doozy of a story about her trip.*

Barbara began, "You know he is the first non-Italian Pope, and I had the privilege of having dinner with him years ago when he was just a Cardinal."

"Wow, that's exciting," I commented. "Now, I remember you telling me that your pastor invited his friend Cardinal Karol Wojtyla to visit Buffalo long before there was any notion that he would become John Paul II."

Backtracking, Barbara filled me in on the other details of her pilgrimage. "We sat in horrible traffic as caravans of busses headed to Canada. The ninety-minute trip took five hours. After we arrived, the bus we chartered parked in a huge muddy field near Toronto. The driver unloaded our belongings and left without saying another word."

Barbara continued, "No one prepared us adequately for the reality of this journey. I thought to bring a folding chair and a backpack with some warm clothing, but none of us were equipped for being outside for hours."

She explained that they were already mud-spattered, and her group was stunned when they realized they would be spending the night in this field along with thousands of worshipers.

"Where is our bus?" Barbara asked the director.

Trying to avoid confrontation, the director answered, "Unfortunately, no one seems to know."

The church director made no other accommodations in advance, so they were stranded, waiting in the torrents of rain to see His Holiness. As night fell, the temperature began to drop while the pouring rain continued. Drenched worshipers felt beyond miserable. The damp inclement weather chilled Barbara, seeping right into her bones. She decided to add some layers of clothing from those nestled in her waterproof backpack. "Thank heaven; my son insisted I bring a raincoat, umbrella, and extra dry clothing."

With no other shelter available, Barbara entered one of the hundreds of porta-potties that dotted her surroundings. Shivering and her teeth chattering uncontrollably, she changed, jumping on one foot and then the other to pull up her pantyhose, determined not to slip on the mud-caked floor. Her wet clothing was stubbornly uncooperative. She had to be a contortionist to complete this task. Victorious, she emerged from the "Johnny on the Spot."

William, a male passenger from her bus, overheard Barbara telling her friends that she was warmer, but balancing while she was changing was quite a challenge. He continued to eavesdrop and was highly amused. He listened as she told her friends, "I'm so fortunate there was a little sink inside so I could keep my purse and backpack off the floor."

He couldn't take it anymore, and his laughter exploded. He finally interrupted, apologizing that he couldn't help overhearing their conversation. Then, he asked, "Didn't you notice there were no faucets on that sink?"

Barbara told me she failed to understand, but the remainder of the group joined his amusement. Then, stifling giggles, a friend explained that her "cute little sink" was the male urinal. Shaking her head in disbelief, Barbara gasped in horror but resisted the urge to clasp the hand that had held her purse over her mouth.

As a new day dawned, the moment they had so patiently anticipated arrived. Like a miracle, the morning brought sunshine, warming the crowd. Barbara explained, "Pope John Paul II was just a speck in the distance as he said Mass, and the crowds bowed their heads in prayer. It was worth the miserable conditions of the pilgrimage."

I glanced down at Barbara's purse and backpack.

Barbara noticed my expression and said, "My fellow bus passengers are still teasing me. They will never let me forget that fateful trip to the outhouse. I assure you that my purse and backpack never made it back to the States. Instead, I tossed them in the bonfire that kept us warm."

6

Wham-O

Barbara arrived for her dental appointment looking as red as a boiled lobster and quite uncomfortable. I admonished her for being so sunburned. Sheepishly, she admitted she had spent the previous afternoon on the roof of her house.

I asked, "What were you doing up there?"

"Guess I should have been more careful," she proclaimed. "I outdid myself this time."

She explained that last week, the neighborhood kids were playing Frisbee. A strong wind gust caught the plastic disc and planted it in the middle of Barbara's roof. After a week of rain and wind, the wayward object clung to the shingles and was not coming down by itself. So Barbara decided to go after it.

I knew Barbara's late husband Walter had made his living as a lineman for the phone company and could never understand her fear of heights. On the other hand, Barbara was terrified and couldn't even watch people in high places. Barbara confessed that she was constantly frustrated when she needed assistance with household maintenance.

With tears in her eyes, she said, "I wish Walter were here. I could have used his help yesterday."

She then laughed as she described the events that led to her blistering sunburn. Barbara told me she planned to visit her son and his wife, who had moved out of state. Barbara admitted the Frisbee was bothering her, and it would drive her crazy to leave town with a yellow disc on the roof.

Barbara had no business climbing a ladder, even if she was pretty agile for a woman in her sixties. Moreover, it was ridiculous since she was terrified of heights and had no idea what she was doing.

She painstakingly dragged a heavy ladder from the garage and looked at it in confusion. She didn't understand the mechanics of the ladder, and she wasn't sure how to place it correctly or set the clips so that the ladder would stay extended. Chuckling, she admitted that was where the story should have ended.

Barbara described her battle with the cumbersome ladder. "I found the ladder difficult to manipulate, and I felt ridiculous jumping on the bottom rung to set the ladder in the grass as I had seen my husband do so many times. Was it at the correct angle? I wondered as I cautiously started climbing up the slippery rungs."

"Barbara, you should have waited till your neighbors were home," I commented.

"I have to admit that I am stubborn and bullheaded. It's just against my nature to ask for help."

I shook my head.

Barbara grunted, "I started up the ladder and was pretty proud of myself, thinking this wasn't so bad. I gingerly planted one foot and then the other on the pitched roof, beaming that I was conquering my fear of heights. Then focusing only on the Frisbee, I let go of the ladder. Instantly, I heard a metal-on-metal scraping noise as the ladder slid sideways, crashing to the ground, landing with a loud thump."

Barbara sat frozen and motionless, trapped on the roof. Her home was a one-story ranch, but she was still twenty feet off the ground. She couldn't believe a child's toy, invented by the toy company Wham-O, could have possibly caused her demise.

A few vehicles had traveled down her street that day. She tried to grab their attention by shouting and waving her arms frantically, but the cars had their windows closed, radios blaring, and air conditioners cranked full blast. No one noticed her plight. Others just gave a friendly wave back.

Barbara sighed, "What a big mistake it was to prop the ladder from the back of the house, hidden from the street."

She thought, "If only I had something to throw at the cars. Ah, the Frisbee!" To get the best leverage, Barbara tried to stand. She panicked as she started to slide. Placing her butt back on the hot shingles, she hurled the disc.

She moaned, "I guess I'm not such a great aim because it sailed in the air, gliding like an eagle, and instead of landing in front of the passing car, it proceeded to land on a neighboring roof."

Releasing a heavy sigh of relief, she saw the school bus coming to drop off the teenage Frisbee owners. Defeated and sunburned, Barbara was humiliated but appreciative to be rescued by the bus driver. The teenagers stopped laughing when they heard their neighbor had been baking in the blistering sun for six hours. They put the ladder away for her. No more ladders, she vowed.

Barbara said with a mischievous glint in her eyes, "I have no idea how I am going to explain this sunburn to my son, but you can be sure there won't be any mention of a ladder or roof."

7

Liberty Bell Blues

I was delighted to see Barbara's name on the dental schedule again. I knew she had a riveting anecdote to share since my daughter was involved. It was difficult not to blurt out the story to my co-workers, but I promised Barbara she could tell it herself.

Over the years, I had become good friends with Barbara's son Walter and his wife Maria, choosing them to be my daughter's godparents. So I arranged for my eleven-year-old daughter Nicole to accompany Barbara on her trip to Pennsylvania.

The couple planned an exciting week of visiting tourist attractions for their guests, including sightseeing in Philadelphia. Their very first stop was the Liberty Bell. Of course, everyone was excited. Moved from Independence Hall to a specially built pavilion, the monument was foremost on their list.

Philly was experiencing a prolonged heat wave, yet the line to see the Liberty Bell snaked around the block. Nicole stood in the oppressive heat until the doors opened but had arrived early enough to procure a front-row spot inside along the velvet ropes that encircled the historical artifact. The frigid air inside the building was a welcome relief as Nicole listened intently to the Park Ranger.

Five minutes into the presentation, Barbara glanced at Nicole and noticed she had turned ghostly pale. My daughter said, "I don't feel so good. The room is spinning."

Nicole went down with a thump, hitting her head on the marble floor. Unexpectedly, she projectile vomited all over the Ranger and most of the exhibition hall. Thankfully, she missed the Liberty Bell, probably because she was prone on the exhibition floor. The crowd gagged and gasped, and throngs hurried out of the building. The Park Ranger's response was to close the pavilion for the rest of the day.

In the meantime, Barbara asked for directions to the nearest hospital. It proved to be a colossal mistake because driving in Philadelphia without a GPS is risky. Barbara found herself traveling the wrong way on one-way streets. There was no turning back when they realized the closest hospital was not in the most desirable part of town.

Nicole began talking incoherently. Barbara drove faster, thinking, "Nicole probably has a head injury. She hit that marble floor hard. I wish I hadn't refused the Ranger's offer to call an ambulance."

They spent the following eight hours in a crowded emergency room while I waited helplessly, three hundred miles away, clutching the phone, desperate for news from Barbara. It would have been wonderful if there was such a thing as a cell phone. Instead, I had to make the painstaking decision of waiting by the phone or jumping in the car. The doctor stressed that he needed to be able to reach me to discuss treatment options. There was no choice but to stay home.

After numerous tests and X-rays, there was no confirmed diagnosis. Thankfully, the medicines made Nicole feel better. The doctors speculated that Nicole, a prepubescent adolescent girl, was overcome by dramatic temperature changes, triggering this violent reaction.

When the doctor ordered her release from the emergency room, her dad and I jumped in the car and drove the six hours to Allentown. We couldn't wait to hold her in our arms, yet we couldn't resist teasing her about single-handily closing down a national monument.

8

Bumper Carts

After a long day at work, I stopped at the grocery store to pick up a few items. I didn't realize it would be such a bad idea.

Hazel, a long-time patient of mine, was on a motorized store scooter, frantically waving, trying to get my attention. "Yoo-hoo, Terry, Helloo," she shouted. "It's my first time on one of these contraptions." When I heard her, I was balancing in a crouched position, trying to retrieve an item from the bottom shelf.

I glanced up to see Hazel heading straight for me. She surged forward, ramming my basket that was between me and the scooter. The momentum of the cart shoved me to the ground. I plopped on my butt and pinned against the shelf on the sticky floor. I looked up in astonishment.

Slam, boom, bang, the scooter hit my cart repeatedly. I couldn't move or get out of the way. I took a direct hit each time the scooter collided with my cart. Hazel became frantic as the out-of-control vehicle lurched forward. She kept repeating, "I'm sorry. I'm so sorry."

I was trapped as the inexperienced operator walloped another forceful thump into me. Hazel tried to stop the beast of a machine, but the harder she tried, the worse it got.

I yelled, "Put it in reverse!"

Trying desperately to comply, she inadvertently jammed the controls locked in forward. Hazel kept ramming me like a bumper car in an amusement park. She was now hysterical. "These darn cataracts. I can't read the controls," she cried.

I pleaded, "Take your hands off the controls. Stop! Turn it off."

Nearby, shopping on the next aisle, Hazel's husband heard a commotion. As he rounded the corner, he saw the ridiculous scene. I was on the floor while Hazel bounced in her seat as the defiant vehicle kept attacking.

By this time, a crowd had gathered. Approaching Hazel from behind, her husband grabbed the switch and turned off the ignition. To be heard above her blubbering, he shouted, "Don't touch a thing! Just sit there." Looking at her sympathetically, he added, "Honey, it will be ok."

Hurrying to help me up, he asked, "Are you hurt? I can see black and blue marks forming on your shins."

"I'm a little dirty and embarrassed, but I'm fine," I tried reassuring them. Hazel was practically inconsolable, and I knew she must be so humiliated.

Her husband said, "This is entirely my fault. Since her knee replacement, maneuvering with a walker has been exhausting for her. I told her the store scooter would give her more independence. What was I thinking, encouraging her to use this motorized monster?"

Finding it difficult to stop crying, Hazel sniveled but managed to apologize. "Can you forgive me?"

I reassured her, "It will be fine, Hazel." Then I lied, "It could have happened to anyone." Feeling battered and bruised, I thought *someone should outlaw those things unless you pass a road test!*

As I rushed to get away from the crazy driver, I heard Hazel tell her husband in a hushed tone, "I hope she doesn't take it out on me when she cleans my teeth. You know, she uses all those sharp instruments!"

9

A Bleary-Eyed Whimsical Vision

I had not seen Hazel since my encounter with her motorized shopping cart that shoved me to the ground in the "bumper-carts" incident until the day she had a dental appointment with me.

She sat in the waiting room with her eyes cast down. Then, sheepishly, Hazel followed me to the treatment room. She confessed that she had postponed her appointment because she was embarrassed to face me.

"I've forgotten all about it," I lied.

Hazel quickly responded, "I hope you don't hold a grudge. You do use all those sharp instruments."

As I updated her medical history, Hazel said, "You will be thrilled to know I had my cataracts done. It became an urgent necessity! I had no choice because after I ran you down, another situation made me realize it was time for the surgery."

Hazel told me she picked up her friend Jackie to run some errands in an unfamiliar part of town. "We were exasperated because we were stuck in traffic, driving behind a mass transit bus. The fumes were killing us."

For once, they were glad to be stuck at a red light since the bus continued ahead. Hazel told me she kept staring at the bus stop on the next corner.

Hazel asked Jackie, "What do you think is going on? I have never seen so many people waiting for a bus!"

Shaking her head, Jackie kept glancing ahead at the corner and asked, "What do you mean? Are we looking at the same corner?"

Hazel answered in a confused tone, "Don't you see the people at the bus stop? It looks like about a hundred of them crowded near the street. I wonder why the nearly empty bus didn't stop."

Hazel explained that Jackie looked at her with a perplexed expression. Then, she said, "I couldn't understand what was wrong. Jackie acted like I was crazy. I pleaded with her to clue me in. What's so funny?"

Jackie hooted. "Honestly, Hazel, I have no doubt you are way overdue for that cataract surgery. Please stop and let me drive!"

With laughter in her voice, Hazel proceeded to describe the scene. "When we got closer, there was a huge twelve-foot banner from Mistletoe Meadows Tree Farm. No wonder Jackie was confused. Hundreds of Christmas trees, not people, stood in rows by the bus stop."

Alarmed, Hazel pulled the car to the curb. She looked at Jackie, "You're right! I'll call for an eye appointment as soon as we get home."

10

Murdering the Monarch

Gloria, our dental office receptionist, loves every kind of animal, big and small, but has an extreme phobia regarding insects, especially the flying varieties, including harmless ladybugs and beautiful butterflies.

Gloria was excited to accompany her granddaughter Sophie's kindergarten trip to Niagara Falls She told me, "We were both delighted as we boarded the bus in Buffalo, NY, for the forty-five-minute drive across the Canadian border. However, the color drained from my face as the bus pulled into the Butterfly Conservatory parking lot."

"Are you alright, Grandma?" the child asked.

"Why are we here? Aren't we going to see the Falls?"

"No, Grandma, that trip is for first graders. We're going to see the beautiful butterflies."

"Beautiful or not, I don't know if I can do this," Gloria confessed to the teacher.

The teacher replied, "Gloria, we are short two chaperones; I'm afraid you have no choice."

Gathering her courage, Gloria forced a smile as she joined the group for a special private tour. As they entered the rainforest environment, Gloria gulped. It felt like two hundred humid degrees, which proved not very conducive to the monumental hot flash she was experiencing. In contrast, her granddaughter was beaming as she watched the colorful creatures flitting through the air.

Standing behind a glass partition and listening to the tour guide, Gloria mumbled, "I'm glad this viewing area exists. I can handle this."

The perky tour guide proudly explained they housed forty-five species and over two thousand butterflies. "Today, they are especially active; you will find them floating freely among the lush greenery. Now, let's go inside for a close-up look."

In a panic, Gloria looked to the teacher for encouragement. The teacher, absorbed in keeping track of her students, shrugged her shoulders and motioned Gloria ahead. The children were giggling with pleasure as clusters of butterflies flitted all around.

Trudging forward, gripping her granddaughter's hand, Gloria ducked, dodged, and swayed in avoidance as the butterflies milled around her. In Gloria's phobic state of mind, the silent fluttering wings sounded like thousands of buzzing bees in her ears. Little Sophie was embarrassed by the spectacle Grandma Gloria was making of herself.

"Just hold on; this will be over soon," the teacher whispered. "Do you think you could be a little less dramatic? You are scaring the children!"

Twenty heads with innocent eyes turned, glued on the crazy Grandma that seemed to have lost her mind. They were laughing at her reaction to the harmless creatures. The tour guide tried to divert their attention, but at that precise moment, Sophie saw something extraordinary.

Excitedly, she tugged at Gloria's shirt. "Grandma, look, three butterflies just landed in your hair. Aren't they beautiful? Do they tickle?"

Gloria heard nothing after *butterflies* and *hair*. An instinctive reaction took over, causing Gloria to squirm with her arms flailing as she swatted at the butterflies. Smack--whoosh--s-p-l-a-t. An incredibly stunning monarch hit the pavement, landing at Sophie's feet.

The tour guide screamed. She shouted a hysterical jargon, no one could understand, causing twenty kindergarteners to cry in unison.

Sophie looked especially distressed as huge tears rolled down her cheeks. Then, still sniffling, she cried, "Grandma, you killed that pretty butterfly!"

Gloria was speechless. Her mind was trying to compile some intelligent thoughts.

The teacher came to the rescue announcing, "Children, we have a special treat. Grandma Gloria agreed to buy us all ice cream in the cafeteria."

As Gloria paid for the cones, she watched the conservatory curator and a Royal Mounted Police Officer approach her. "This can't be good," Gloria thought.

In a stern voice, the officer said, "Excuse me, ma'am, but you will have to come with me."

He pulled Gloria aside from the group. He said, "I have to inform you that we are banning you from ever visiting here again!"

Gloria's voice trembled. "Do you mean Canada?"

The Mountie's eyes softened as he said, "No, Ma'am. I mean the Butterfly Conservatory."

Filled with relief, Gloria pulled out her checkbook to write a generous donation to the Canadian Horticultural Society that nurtures the butterflies.

Twenty exhausted kindergarteners boarded the bus. They each closed their eyes and were fast asleep before even pulling out of the parking lot, except Sophie, who was teary-eyed and glaring at Grandma.

Gloria felt terrible. She put her arm around her granddaughter, thinking, *Sophie would probably be in college before she forgave me, and this grandma would never be asked on a field trip again.*

Unexpectedly, with forgiving eyes, little Sophie looked up at Grandma Gloria and said, "It's okay, Grandma; I know old people can't help it."

11

A Stone Cold Mystery

Carol came into her dental appointment still jet-lagged. I said, "How was your trip? I can't wait to hear all about Russia."

I knew Carol and Nan had been friends all their lives, and now they are steadfast traveling companions in their retirement. Their "Lucy and Ethel" escapades were always a hoot, but this one was closer to resembling a Sherlock Holmes mystery.

Carol began, "As the first day ended, completely and utterly exhausted, we looked forward to a hot shower and a comfy bed. We had to trudge up eight flights of stairs to a tiny room with only a common restroom at the end of each hall. Not exactly the Ritz."

After a sleepless night, Carol rose, showered, and dressed. She told Nan, "Please hurry. I'll wait outside to flag down the tour bus." Carol descended the stairs lugging a tote bag filled with necessities for the day. She reached the fourth-floor landing, and noticed the stairwell door was ajar.

Carol felt the adrenaline rush as she slowly opened the door. Staring at the beautiful stilettos peeking onto the platform, Carol thought the woman had fallen, but she looked oddly still. Carol was starting to panic, but she poked her, asking, "Are you all right?"

The frantic pounding on the door annoyed Nan. "You are so very impatient!" Nan scolded. Carol stood with wildly quivering lips, whimpering uncontrollably. Carol shouted, "Come with me!" Loud sobs made her impossible to understand. "Come with me!" she cried again.

With a white-knuckled grip, Carol grabbed Nan's arm, trying to drag her downstairs. Calmly, Nan unclasped the clammy hands from her wrist. Nan continued, "Carol, you tend to overreact. We'll figure it out." Nan assumed they just missed the bus. Stammering, Carol tried to explain, "I found... I found... uh, I f-o-u-n-d a woman dead in the hallway."

Skeptical of what Carol had witnessed, Nan hurried down the stairs alone to disprove Carol's claims. Nan bolted, covering her mouth to suppress the screams, leaping up the stairs two at a time. "You were right! What should we do?" They held each other, shuddering, trying to determine the next logical step.

Carol shrieked, "Let's try knocking on neighboring rooms." No one answered as they tried to summon help. Fearfully, they descended the flights, holding hands. Nan said, "I hope the body is gone. Maybe we were mistaken."

Unfortunately, this was not their imagination. Still jutting out the door, the woman's legs blocked the landing. Gingerly stepping over the corpse, the duo ran out into the street, attempting to flag down a motorist.

They saw the tour bus approaching. The driver opened the door, and Carol and Nan were incoherently screaming in unison, "Help, help, we need help!" The driver's first instinct was to slam the doors shut, and he was tempted to drive away. Seeing the obligatory tour name tags on their shirts, he was required to stop. "Ladies, ladies, what seems to be the problem?"

"We found a dead woman. There is a body in the hall!" they exclaimed. The burly bus driver parked, stepped out, and closed the door so fellow passengers couldn't hear the commotion. He told Carol and Nan, "Stay put. I will check myself." Carol and Nan stood frozen, waiting for his return.

Slowly approaching, the driver clasped his hands over his worried and perspiring face. "Ladies, you can't go back in there! Get on the bus!" His mobile phone connected him to a police sergeant he knew. Speaking in hushed tones, "You better send a car over to…," he relayed.

Nan asked, "Can you hear what he is saying?" Carol responded, "What does it matter? I don't speak Russian!"

"Quickly, ladies, please get on the bus," the driver instructed. "Locking the bus door, he wiped his brow with a blue bandana, and completely ignored Carol and Nan's insistence for answers.

Sternly, the driver said, "It is imperative for us to leave!" The two naïve tourists protested loudly as the bus pulled away. "Shouldn't we wait to talk to the police?" they argued. The bus driver knew better. "Ladies, it is important to pretend you saw nothing. Don't discuss this with anyone. Lips must be sealed."

I was spellbound by Carol's account, "Then what happened?"

She told me since they were in Russia, they felt it prudent to abide by the wisdom of the bus driver. "News broadcasts often air horror stories of Americans getting caught up in some criminal activity in a foreign country," Nan scolded.

Carol replied, "At the very least, I think we should demand an explanation from the bus driver." Instead of answering, the driver started a cassette of pre-recorded tour information describing the historic buildings around them.

It was the beginning of the second day of their trip, yet they could not enjoy a single moment of the incredible sights. After the day-long tour, there was still a bustle of police activity when they returned to the hotel. Carol said, "Nan, I don't care how much money we lose. I can never go back in there." The terrified tourists pleaded with the bus driver. He finally relented, agreeing to collect their belonging from their room. Handing over the key, they waited on the now-empty bus. "I'll drive you to another location for the night," he offered.

The bus driver explained, "I immediately recognized the body. She has been linked to a corrupt government scandal. The news has been full of this coverage. It was best to stay anonymous."

Flabbergasted, Carol remarked, "This is definitely an encounter right out of the Twilight Zone."

12

A Sparkling Celebration

Our family wanted to surprise my father-in-law with a rip-roaring sixty-fifth birthday party. Strategy for the get-together was taking shape, but the real challenge would be finding the perfect gift. The brainstorming began.

My husband said, "How about a belly dancer? We're always teasing Dad about his 'hardship duty' during WWII, where he often dined at the Sultan's palace in Morocco, enjoying troupes of gorgeous women."

I laughed, "Hiring a belly dancer will embarrass him to death! Let's do it!"

We set the date, ordered the food, picked out the cake, and invited the guests. Arriving at the appointed time, a caravan of vehicles clogged the quiet street. A high fence blocked the view, and right on schedule, fifty people, carrying brightly wrapped packages, paraded into the backyard yelling surprise.

My unsuspecting in-laws were startled. When the party was in full swing, we patiently waited for the belly dancer to arrive. Our video cameras were close at hand.

We noticed the dancer was already half an hour late, and Papa insisted he wanted cake. After an hour passed, we realized there would be no shimmies, spins, or backbends at this party. Everyone was disappointed that our plan was spoiled.

To keep the party moving, I brought out the sheet cake. Since we were outside, someone suggested using sparklers instead of candles. Utter chaos erupted as twenty sparklers, spitting fire, set the tablecloth ablaze. Party decorations on the fence went up in a flash. The flames jumped to the next table. Guests flitted about like the Keystone Cops, trying to smother the fire. These well-intentioned observers only made matters worse, inadvertently fanning the flames. An astute guest quickly grabbed the garden hose before sparks ignited the gift table.

While squelching Grandma's terrified screams, we watched plumes of black smoke fill the air. Once we realized no one was injured, howls of laughter ensued. We had a colossal mess on our hands. Smoldering ashes, falling like snowflakes, swirled in the air as the breeze swept them over the fence.

I turned to my husband, "Do you hear sirens?"

We stopped the firefighters before they pulled out heavy fire hoses and drenched us all. Meticulously, they checked the scene to make sure nothing would rekindle. Mortified, my in-laws apologized to emergency responders. "Sorry, we can't offer you some cake. We drowned it."

As the fire department left, the house phone was ringing. I ran to answer it. "Are you the people that hired the belly dancer for the surprise party?" a shaky voice asked.

I said, "Yes, did you get lost?"

"Oh, mercy, no, this is her mother. She was in a car accident on the way to the party."

I was very concerned. "I hope your daughter wasn't seriously injured."

Her mom answered, "She will be out of commission for a while with a broken leg."

Even without our exotic dancer, the party was a success. My husband captured all the commotion, immortalizing it in a cleverly designed photo collage of flaming tables, firemen, and the horrified expressions on his parent's faces. The party had long passed, but the creative photo in my treatment room helped me relax my patients with this humorous story.

A few weeks later, a new patient hobbled in on crutches with her leg in a cast. She awkwardly maneuvered herself into my dental chair.

"Sorry, I'm having a difficult time getting used to these crutches."

On the medical health form, she filled in the blank for occupation as librarian. She was attractive, impeccably outfitted in tailored clothing, with her hair swept up in a bun but with unflattering horned-rimmed glasses perched on her nose.

I thought *she's the perfect stereotype. The only thing out of place is the crutches.* So I asked about the cast.

She offered, "I had an unfortunate accident."

As we chatted, she asked, "Is that your family?" She seemed intrigued by the photo.

"Yes," I replied with enthusiasm. "Let me tell you the crazy mishaps at that party." Even after telling the story countless times, it was still impossible to keep a straight face. "We had an unintentional bonfire in my father-in-law's backyard after the sparklers set the tables on fire."

She began laughing.

I continued, "At least we had some excitement since our big surprise never showed up."

"What was the surprise?" she asked.

"We hired a belly dancer for the high point of the celebration. Regrettably, that didn't work out. She was in a car wreck and never made it."

My new patient looked pretty astonished and began to giggle. "I'm afraid that might have been me."

I was dumbfounded. "Um, I thought you were a librarian."

"Oh, I am." She explained, "Belly-dancing is a hobby. I was in my costume when a car crashed into me on the way to the party."

Chuckling, the young woman continued, "The EMTs had a field day! They couldn't wait to unload the gurney from the ambulance to see the reaction of the emergency room staff."

We both laughed as I said, "I know my father-in-law would have had stars in his eyes."

13

The Landlord's Surprise

When I chose a career as a dental hygienist, no one warned me I would be a confessor or confidante to so many people. However, over the years, I've observed that fear of the dental chair creates nervous energy that makes some people chatty.

Gracie was terribly upset when she came for her dental appointment. I suggested we postpone it, but she wanted to pour out her horrific experience from earlier in the week. What could I do? I had to listen.

Gracie started rambling. "Maybe you saw it on the news? Oh, my goodness, I never expected to be on the news!" I shook my head because I had no idea what she was talking about.

Gracie told me she manages an apartment complex in an old building without an elevator. Many tenants were seniors, so it was difficult for them, but they continued to live there because it was affordable.

Gracie described a long-time tenant, Mrs. Gibson, as a sweet woman in her eighties who lived in a third-floor apartment for forty years. In the past few years, her nephew Derrick had made himself at home in Auntie's apartment. Derrick always told people he had to work from home since his full-time job was caring for his aunt, and Mrs. Gibson depended on him.

The once temporary arrangement now worked for both of them. It seemed to be a win-win arrangement.

Derrick is nerdy, with horn-rimmed glasses, a comb-over, and his clothes always look rumpled. She continued, "In the three years that he lived in the building, he rarely left the apartment except to grocery shop or to visit the library. He often checked out large print and audiobooks for his aunt. We all thought that was sweet."

She told me that Mrs. Parson, the local branch librarian, is also a tenant in the building. Gracie was now talking faster. She said. "I know the librarian is pretty nosy, and I often dismiss her trivial gossip. Casually, she mentioned that she observed quite a change in Derrick's reading material over the past few years."

"Why should anyone care about that?" I asked her.

"Well," Mrs. Parson said, "He still checks out the large print romance novels that Mrs. Gibson loves, but now he seems to have a fascination with taxidermy and Egyptian mummies, even reserving books from other branches." In addition, the observant librarian noticed she saw him out more often. Gracie continued, "I guess I should have listened more closely, but she is such a busybody that I completely dismissed it."

I groaned, thinking *where in the world is this story going?* "Gracie," I said in a firm tone, "We really have to get started on your cleaning." She completely ignored me and kept talking. I gave up and wondered why this librarian and Derrick upset her so much.

Gracie told me that earlier in the week, she received a complaint from one of the tenants that water was pouring through her ceiling from Mrs. Gibson's apartment.

Gracie knocked and shouted out. Then, using the master key, she let herself into the apartment. The upper flat was unusually quiet except for the sound of running water. It was unbearably hot and stuffy, with a peculiar odor permeating the room.

A creepy feeling crawled up Gracie's spine. She shuddered as she hesitantly moved farther into the room. Gracie rubbed the back of her neck, trying to relieve the tension she felt. "This is silly," she mumbled as she crossed the room.

Not expecting anyone to be home, Gracie was startled when she saw Mrs. Gibson sitting in the rocking chair in the dimly lit room.

With a shaky voice, she said, "Oh, Mrs. Gibson, you frightened me."

Gracie didn't know why she had such an uneasy feeling. "It's so dark in here. Do you mind if I turn on the light?" Gracie didn't wait for an answer as she turned on the light in the darkened room.

Gracie jerked her head back, and her hands covered her mouth as a high-pitched scream escaped her lips. In the rocking chair sat Mrs. Gibson's shriveled mummified remains. Gracie's face turned ashen as she ran from the apartment, shrieking. Well, now Gracie had my undivided attention.

She told me it felt like she stepped into a horror movie. Gracie forgot about the water leak as she called the police.

Not everything is always as they seem. Derrick turned out to be a criminal. The once saintly nephew had been reading books on the mummifying process so he could preserve his dear aunt to continue collecting her social security checks.

Gracie turned to me. Still shaken from the experience of two days before, she said, "Derrick won't have to worry about expenses anymore because he will be spending a lot of time in prison." She also added, "I gave my notice as the apartment manager. Let me know if you know of any jobs."

I laughed and told her we were looking for a good-natured receptionist. "Are you interested? You can have the employee discount since we never did clean your teeth today."

14

Breaking Tradition

My first job as a hygienist was working for Dr. Susan Bliss, a prominent dentist in Buffalo, New York. I was thrilled to be hired into a thriving dental practice.

Dr. Bliss was overjoyed when her son announced his engagement. But, being the groom's mother, she was disappointed not to be included in the wedding planning.

She told me, "I guess I have to respect the old adage that the mother of the groom just needs to show up and wear beige."

I said, "You look horrible in beige." We both laughed.

My boss told me she was to have dinner with the bride and her parents. Susan later informed me that she felt so much better after their evening. "Oh, the good news is the bride's mother told me she was wearing beige and I could choose any other color. Isn't that great?"

"That's a relief," I chuckled.

"There's more," she continued, "The bride requests absolutely no photographs allowed in church during the ceremony, but I think they'll regret it when they look back."

"I couldn't agree more," I said.

The long-awaited day of the wedding arrived. Susan's gown was a pale shade of ice blue with a hint of gray. It was stunning. But when the families met in the church vestibule, the bride and both mothers shrieked.

Susan practically screamed, "You said you were wearing beige!"

The bride's mother burst into tears, "I changed my mind."

The mood became very unsettling. The two mothers had identical dresses, right down to the color, but unfortunately, it was too late to remedy the situation. It ruined the lighthearted mood of the wedding party, but they had to move on as the wedding processional began playing, and they were to be seated.

The groom's brother, who was a priest, officiated the ceremony, making the day extra special. Since the couple felt the cameras disrupted the formality of the marriage ceremony, there wasn't a photographer to capture the next bizarre event.

As everyone turned their heads, watching the bride being escorted down the aisle by both her mother and father, I caught something out of the corner of my eye. I cringed as I saw a wino entering through the side door. Filthy, in a tattered coat and ski cap, he strolled down the side aisle, making his way to the altar. I was trying to figure out a way to have him escorted out.

I turned to my husband, "What do we do? I hope he doesn't cause trouble."

As the bride reached the altar, the uninvited intruder plopped himself next to the lectern on the side altar. He made no sounds. He didn't cause a fuss. He just sat with his crinkled brown bag, sipping his wine.

Everyone fixated on the potentially explosive situation unfolding to the left of the main altar. However, the priest had a good poker face. He proceeded with the wedding rituals as if everything was normal. The wedding party sat in the first pew with a ring-side seat, while the bride and groom had no idea what was happening to the side of them.

People in the church seemed frozen, unsure of what to do. I was desperately trying to think of a discreet way to make the wino leave without causing a commotion. The priest kept calm and purposely positioned the couple to exchange vows with their backs to the side altar. Muffled whispers filled the church, as in horror, the guests watched the wino rise from his seat. He was headed right for the bride and groom when, thankfully, he did an about-face, staggering out the exact route he followed entering the church.

Again, the priest strategically positioned the couple and announced, "You may kiss your bride."

Thunderous applause erupted as the couple shared their first kiss, and the wino exited. Little did the newlywed know most of the applause was for the departing uninvited guest.

I whispered to my husband, "Please follow him out and make sure he leaves."

The priest did a great job of keeping the wedding service flowing. When the ceremony was over, and the happy couple turned to the congregation, they were oblivious to the drama that had taken place. They seemed to float down the aisle to the back of the church, forming a receiving line to share their excitement with the family and guests.

As the newlyweds emerged from the church, everyone opened their bags of rice to toss at the couple. The wino was waiting on the church stairs grabbing and hugging the guests. He went from one pretty woman to the next.

I shoved my husband over towards him before he grabbed the bride. "I told you to get rid of him!"

He shrugged his shoulders and said, "I thought I did!"

Astonished, the bride saw the wino making himself at home in the crowd. She was so blissfully happy that neither the dress fiasco nor the homeless man could ruin her day.

I overheard some guests chattering. "Wasn't it ingenious having the mothers wear the same dress? I bet they planned that for color balance in the wedding portraits."

I looked at my husband and said, "Wow, if they only knew! Do you think anyone got a picture of the wino? I can't wait to talk to Susan; she looks very pale."

15

The Imperfect-Perfect Wedding

Dr. Pulchaski, my boss, was very fortunate to have Helena as his receptionist. Born and raised in this predominantly Polish community, Helena inherited her family home, where she chose to raise six children. As a result, Helena knew everyone in this section of the city. The dental practice thrived because of her compassionate interactions and familiarity with the patient's extended family.

One day, Helena arrived at work floating on cloud nine. Her daughter's visit home last week had been to announce her engagement. As a mother of five sons, Helena expressed excitement that she and Claire, her only daughter, could plan a wedding together. However, Helena confided in me that the groom was New York society and feared the wedding wouldn't be in Buffalo.

"It pains me that Claire has always been embarrassed by her Polish heritage and the neighborhood where she grew up. She escaped by going to New York City for college and Boston for Law School. I'm ashamed to say she has become quite the snob," Helena confessed.

Claire told her mother, "My dream wedding would be at Saint Patrick's Cathedral, followed by a ride to the reception in a gorgeous horse-drawn carriage."

After seeing her mother's pained expression, Claire reluctantly convinced her fiancé they could have the same lavish wedding at her parish church. However, Claire absolutely refused to have a mundane reception in the church hall with a polka band. Helena couldn't afford alternative arrangements nor understood the need for such extravagance. So the couple readily agreed to pay for everything themselves, which also assured they would determine the venue of their choosing.

A wedding planner with a reputation for meticulous attention to detail directed the preparations. Claire's twelve bridesmaids flew to New York City to choose dresses. On the bride's insistence, Helena's mother-of-the-bride dress was custom-made. A prominent designer created a one-of-a-kind wedding gown for Claire, featuring a cathedral train and a veil that was even longer, cascading down her back. In this close-knit neighborhood, this extravagance was unheard of in 1970.

The bride was out of control, and the money spent was obscene. Helena was uncomfortable and told her daughter it would look like the circus had come to town. "Maybe the wedding should be in New York City," she told Claire.

Tensions were high, and Claire threw it in her mom's face, "I'm having the wedding in Buffalo to appease you, so we'll do it my way!" They were butting heads. It seemed no one was satisfied.

The nosey neighbor gossip mill had been buzzing for months. Nothing of this magnitude had ever taken place in this neighborhood. On the morning of the wedding, a crowd of curious uninvited guests lined the sidewalk with lawn chairs outside the church.

The wait was worthwhile for the excited on-lookers. Hours before the ceremony, two cargo vans arrived, filled with topiary trees. The magnificent shrubberies were placed along the church steps, making a park-like path for the bride to walk through. As those trucks pulled away, two more arrived, carrying more flowers, bows, and ribbons to decorate the pews. Helena felt the exorbitant display exhibited over-the-top pretentiousness. Embarrassed, she had no idea how she would hold her head up with her neighbors.

The wedding planner had ordered a pricey hansom cab to be pulled by two white horses. The newlyweds emerged from the church, stood on the top stair, and released two white doves, a sight the crowd had never seen before.

When the bride looked at the street, her mouth was agape. "This can't be happening!" Claire screamed and fainted into her groom's arms.

Instead of the gorgeous, Cinderella-like carriage, waiting at the curb was a grimy buckboard wagon. Perched on the only seat was a man dressed in a plaid flannel shirt, dirty jeans, cowboy boots, and a hat with a piece of alfalfa dangling from his mouth.

When Claire opened her eyes, she gasped, "All the money we spent, all the planning and attention to detail, everything is falling apart. My carefully planned wedding is turning into a monumental disaster." She shouted, "Where's the wedding planner?"

When Claire thought matters couldn't get worse, the skies opened up in a torrential downpour that came out of nowhere, drenching everyone.

Dr. Pulchalski, watching the distraught bride, saved the day. He brought his Cadillac around and offered it to the newlyweds. Most of the guests saw the humor of the situation, and by the end of the reception, even Claire's spirit had lifted.

Helena had tears in her eyes as Claire said, "Mom if I hadn't tried to outdo everyone, this never would have happened."

Claire's tears turned to giggles as she hugged her mom. The bride shrugged her shoulders and said, "I envisioned a fairytale wedding; instead, I got a scene from the Wild West."

16

Polka Dots-Oh My!

My husband and I attended a beautiful wedding ceremony for the daughter of one of my patients. The reception, filled with Polish traditions, included the time-honored ritual of unveiling the bride.

Stella, the bride's mother, stood next to me as the polka band's accordion player instructed the guests to form a tight circle around the bride and groom. Stella explained that the song was about twelve angels.

She told us, "Each verse predicts a part of the future life of the newlywed couple. Then, at a specific point in the song, the sixth angel tells how the bride is now a wife, leaving her parents and bonding with her husband. At that precise moment, the maid-of-honor removes the veil and places a little crown on the bride's head. The ballad is very emotional, triggering tears in the womenfolk."

I hugged my patient, Stella, and said, "I'm so glad you explained and translated those Polish lyrics."

Stella smiled, adding, "Poor Lance is probably trying to figure out what's happening, but we purposely failed to inform him about this tradition."

I laughed as I saw a ridiculous hat on the groom. "What's happening now?" I asked. "Lance looks like he doesn't have a clue what is happening."

"He doesn't!" Stella said. "The outrageous hat, covered with props, is really the star of the show. The more things that swing, sway, droop or protrude from the hat, the funnier it becomes."

I stared at the cowboy hat with miniature baby bottles swinging from the wide-brim, a matchbox-size plastic motorcycle, and numerous other tchotchkes with significant meanings to the couple. It was the likes of something I had never seen.

My husband and I watched as the young couple twirled around the dance floor, but I noticed that the bride looked concerned. Then, as they danced past us, I heard the bride ask, "Lance, why do you keep looking at your uncle? You seem preoccupied since the dancing began."

While looking over his shoulder, trying to watch Uncle Buddy, Lance answered, "I should have warned you."

The bride smiled. "Why are you so nervous? I love that man! He runs the best gin mill in town. He reminds me of W.C. Fields with his chubby face and pocked-marked red nose."

A few songs later, the incredibly nervous-looking groom saw Uncle Buddy enter the dance floor. "Oh, not today! I knew it was inevitable that Uncle Bud wouldn't miss his golden opportunity," Lance fretted.

"What are you talking about?" the bride asked.

"My favorite uncle is a great bartender with a booming business because he knows how to spin a story to keep his patrons interested and the beer flowing. But what he does at a wedding has me worried."

The groom's relatives knew what to expect and began crowding around Uncle Bud while the bride's family watched in bewilderment. Then, taking the cue from the groom's side of the family, everyone flooded the dance floor. Apparently, Uncle Bud was famous at every wedding for pulling down his pants and dancing the Hokey Pokey in his red, yellow and blue polka dot boxer shorts resembling the Wonder Bread bag markings.

As I watched in amusement, Stella said, "I just learned this is Uncle Bud's signature move after he is somewhat inebriated."

I said, "His antics trigged all these hoots and hollers. Oh, look! Dollar bills are flying everywhere, earmarked for the young couple."

My husband was laughing as hard as I was. He turned to me and said, "Oh my, that image will be branded in my mind forever! Uncle Bud's three-hundred pounds with a beer-belly gut put a whole new dimension to the Hokey Pokey as we watch him shake it all about."

PART TWO

Rochester, New York

1980-2005

17

Frozen In Time

When I walked into my job interview in Rochester, New York, the pungent antiseptic smell, so typical of a dental office, immediately struck me. In addition, the décor was surprisingly antiquated. I looked around. This office felt like it was frozen in time, and I doubted if this dental practice would fit me well.

Brown walnut paneling covered every wall in the waiting room and reception area. The five-room office, squished into eight hundred square feet, seemed even smaller with this sea of darkness.

I noticed a real treasure on the wall: an old-fashioned black rotary-dial phone. To make a call, you place a finger in the hole corresponding with each number in the phone listing. After rotating the dial to the top, you had to remove your finger so it could automatically return to its original position. With each phone number, you repeated the action six more times.

Prominently sitting on the desk was a yellow manual typewriter. The secretary told me that patients in the waiting room often tried to identify the unfamiliar rhythmic clicking sound coming from behind the partition. Then she said, "One day, the typewriter quit working. I was hoping for an upgrade, but never fear, Dr. Richards had an identical one in his closet at home."

I laughed.

She continued, "I get tickled when a salesman tries to sell us a computer. I point to the rotary phone, and he gets the message."

I was disappointed because I was expecting a modern, up-to-date office, and skeptical since this was unlike any other office or job interview I ever had. Moreover, I was stunned when the first thing my potential employer, Dr. Richards, said was, "Oh, good, you're not so young!"

I was speechless since I was thirty and unsure how to take that comment. We were barely introduced when he asked, "Are you planning on having any more kids?"

I understood his question when he explained that the hygienist he recently hired was quitting because she was expecting. In 1980, you could still ask personal questions in interviews.

My initial tour included focusing on the room where I would be working, called an operatory. I was delighted to see it was brighter, covered in wallpaper. This no-frills office had two treatment rooms, one for the dentist and one for the hygienist.

I cringed when I saw that the dental chairs were identical to the archaic ones I used in dental hygiene school. They didn't recline, and only the headrest was adjustable, forcing the hygienist to be a contortionist, standing in twisted, back-breaking positions for an entire workday. The only difference was the chairs were modern enough to push a button to raise and lower the position, whereas the chairs in school had a foot pedal to pump to adjust the height.

The cute little sink called a cuspidor was attached to the dental unit, where patients could swish and spit to their heart's delight. The water ran continually, swirling around the bowl, flushing away debris. Modern dental units use suction the entire time because rinsing is often a stall technique patients use to keep us from putting our hands back in their mouths.

Another relic was the slow-speed handpiece, which had a belt-driven operating system. Since I stood while I worked, it would be a miracle not to get my hair caught in the belt. Also, a clunky, heavy foot-controlled pedal that operated the tooth polishing device was on the floor beside the chair. I knew it was an obstacle I could trip over.

Lastly, I noticed a lack of a high-speed ultrasonic scaler to make my job easier. The absence of high-tech equipment meant tedious scraping tartar off teeth by hand with sharp, pointed instruments. I thought *Oh, my aching wrists!*

Unlike today, the appointment book was open on the desk for all to see. No HIIPPA (Health Information Patient Privacy Act) existed to demand the hiding of patients' names. Dr. Richards explained his workday ended at 3:00 pm, but I noticed his appointment book showed patients scheduled until 5:00 pm.

I was about to ask about the discrepancy when he explained that his wife was attending law school, and he had to be home for his four children. Dr. Richards clarified, "Fake patient names filled those prime timeslots each week. People are always looking at the scheduling book upside down or over your shoulder, so when someone requests a later-in-the-day appointment, we can justify that they were in demand and booked for months."

Similarly, the summer schedule was a masterpiece. Dr. Richards moved his family to their camp on the St. Lawrence River for the entire school vacation. He commuted from the North Country and only worked three days every other week. Patients assumed Dr. Richards always had a full schedule. Sometimes, they complained but never caught on.

My interview lasted an hour, and I was amused by this odd man. When Dr. Richards felt the salary I requested was too low, he insisted on paying me much more. Now I knew I wanted this job more than ever.

As the interview concluded, Dr. Richards wrote out a check for an hour of my time. To this day, I have never heard of anyone leaving a job interview with a paycheck. That paycheck was the first of many, as we worked together for twenty-five extraordinary years.

18

The Diet Guru

Working for Dr. Richards was never dull since he's well-known as a world-class practical joker in the dental community.

The cleverest hoax Dr. Richards devised was his famous weight loss challenge between his longtime employee Regina and himself. Like most of us, they were constantly battling their weight, and it didn't help that patients frequently brought in home-baked goods. The devious dentist proposed a challenge that the winner with the most weight loss in a month would take the loser's family out to a nice dinner. Naturally, patients encouraged them, and soon we had our own version of the Biggest Loser competition.

After setting the ground rules, they marched into the office of the internist in our building, Dr. Johnson. At the preliminary weigh-in, the nurse made an official chart. Regina was confident that this was assurance that there was no possible way Dr. Richards could cheat.

Regina was not too thrilled with the wager. Dr. Richards had a wife and four children, including two strapping teenage boys who could eat a week's worth of groceries in one sitting, while Regina and her husband had two petite daughters who ate like birds. Optimistic, Regina thought, "I have to win this bet."

Tempted by delicious smells from the break room, especially all the chocolate, she passed up the parade of goodies while Dr. Richards constantly indulged. Instead, she chanted her mantra, "A minute on the lips: forever on the hips." Regina's new determination kept her focused.

With only a month to lose weight, Regina resigned to let the starvation begin. There would be a weekly weigh-in, and Dr. Johnson agreed to be the judge.

It's common knowledge that men lose weight faster than women, but the outcome of the first week's results was astounding. Dr. Richards lost ten pounds. Regina was in a panic. How could she compete with that weight loss? She had only lost two pounds.

"What am I going to do?" Regina started going to the gym daily and was so sore she could hardly eat or do her job. This contest challenged her grit.

At the second weight check, Dr. Richards was down another ten pounds, and as the month progressed, Dr. Richards lost another three. Regina still was nowhere close to twenty-three pounds in a month.

Dr. Richards gloated. He was the winner and undoubtedly the diet guru. He boasted that he was, indeed, the Biggest Loser.

On the night the champ collected his reward, he purposely chose one of the most expensive restaurants in town. The doctor and his wife ordered wine and appetizers, and his whole family ordered costly entrees.

Regina saw dollar signs swimming before her eyes while her brain panicked. She was trying to figure out how many paychecks this would eat.

As predicted, an astronomical figure appeared as the total when the waiter presented her with the check. Regina looked very pale while she wondered if she had even brought enough money because she didn't own a credit card.

Upon seeing Regina's expression as she held the check in her hands, the entire group, including Regina's family, burst out laughing. Thinking that this was very cruel, Regina's eyes brimmed with tears.

Mrs. Richards came to the rescue, telling her husband this had gone far enough. "Fess up," she said.

Earlier in the day, Dr. Richards called Regina's husband to disclose his scheme. It was now time to tell Regina before she had a coronary.

Dr. Richards confessed that he needed to establish a heavier baseline weight at the beginning of the challenge, so he deliberately cheated at the first weigh-in. Discreetly hidden under his lab coat, Dr. Richards wore two heavy lead shield aprons.

He took off one apron at the second weigh-in, resulting in a ten-pound loss. Then, he shed the remaining ten-pound shield at the third scale encounter.

Regina should have realized that this was a setup from the start and that her boss would find a way to outwit her. Thankfully, Dr. Richards picked up the dinner tab, as he had intended to do all along.

19

Secret Admirer

Dr. Richards was a fabulous dentist but also the king of practical jokers. He pranked the staff, his patients, and even his poor children had to be on constant alert.

Our office manager, Mrs. Sperry, was in her late sixties. She recently lost her husband and was reluctant to retire because working with our patients gave her a purpose. The lighthearted atmosphere of the office made her willing to put up with Dr. Richards's shenanigans and sometimes sneaky pranks, but she never expected to become the next target.

Mrs. Sperry noticed a patient, Mr. Crabtree, was due to arrive shortly. It was our first day back at work after a holiday weekend, making our schedule unusually busy.

Turning towards me, she sighed, "He hasn't been here for years. I had secretly nicknamed him "Mr. Crabby." He will have a fit if kept waiting."

I said, "I remember that he was difficult and argumentative at each one of his dental visits. He always had a scowl on his face and barked orders. I'm sure not looking forward to cleaning his teeth."

His oral examination revealed that he had neglected his mouth and required extensive dental treatment. Observing

Mrs. Sperry's interaction with this patient gave Dr. Richards an idea, and his scheming, creative juices began flowing.

Unbeknownst to Mr. Crabtree or Mrs. Sperry, Dr. Richards devised a plan to make her think that this man was her secret admirer. After each appointment, Mrs. Sperry would get a love note in the mail, and she even received a mushy Valentine's card. The candy and flowers delivered to the office astonished her on her birthday, but everything was just signed, your secret admirer.

Dr. Richards went as far as having someone from another office address the envelopes so she wouldn't recognize his handwriting. He made sure something always arrived the day after Mr. Crabtree had an appointment so that Mrs. Sperry couldn't mistake that he was the sender.

Mrs. Sperry was dumbfounded. She said, "He never says a single word to me, except how much do I owe? I'm too embarrassed to acknowledge the gifts, and I don't care for that man one bit."

I commented, "I noticed how beet red you turned today when he walked in the door."

"I know," she said. "I'm beginning to have heart palpitations when I get too close to him. When he's in the dental chair, and I'm assisting, I feel clumsy and all thumbs."

Crabtree usually paid cash for his visits, but as he was leaving this particular day, he handed Mrs. Sperry an envelope addressed to the office that he had forgotten to mail. The handwriting was illegible, chicken scrawl, not bearing any resemblance to the mail she'd been receiving.

After he left, Mrs. Sperry turned to me and said, "I can hardly read his handwriting." Suddenly, a light bulb went off. She whispered, "I think Dr. Richards is pranking me, and he's sending me this stuff."

"No, he wouldn't do that," I said. "Or would he?"

Mrs. Sperry confronted our boss, who couldn't keep a straight face. She made the sign of the cross. "I should be mad at you, but I'm so relieved it was never Mr. Crabtree showing me affection."

Dr. Richards said, "I'm so sorry. You're such a good sport! Unfortunately, I guess I got a little carried away this time."

20

Embrace the Present

Sometimes, I wonder how I even manage to do an oral hygiene exam on certain people. Some patients, who require extra time to clean their teeth, chat non-stop. You would think another hygienist would understand, but my co-worker, Regina, came strolling into the dental office Monday morning, cradling a photo album under her arm. She was having her teeth cleaned on her day off.

For months, Regina had been making banners, decorations, and silk-flower centerpieces for her mom's one-hundredth birthday. I knew she had just returned from her trip home, but I was hoping to hear about the festivities at lunch one day, not in the middle of a cleaning appointment.

As she opened the photo album, Regina told me the story. "My mom, Berta, is considered the matriarch of our small hometown in Vermont. I would bet that every single person who had ever lived there showed up for the party."

"That's terrific!" I said. "That's what keeps your mother young."

Regina and her sisters planned for months to have a massive celebration for their mom's big day. This year, the birth date fell on a Sunday, which was perfect. "After the morning service, we invited the worshippers to join the festivities in the annex building, which was the only place in the entire town that was large enough to accommodate all the guests."

Regina said, "I wish I had half the spunk Mom still has! Friends that are my age are already having cognitive difficulties. I hope I age with at least half my mom's grace and attitude."

I listened as Regina told me they had their birthday gift delivered to the church hall. Guests cheered as the daughters wheeled out a cart with a giant red bow draped across their unwrapped present. It was a motorized recliner that would slowly raise Berta from seated to standing at the push of a button.

Berta looked confused as the sisters eased Mom into the comfy leather chair and began giving lessons. Up, down, back, as the sisters ooo-ed and ahh-ed, showing Mom all the positions.

Berta pleaded, "Stop! Please Stop! Girls, this is making me dizzy."

"My mom has a mind of her own!!" Regina said. "We were so excited, and everyone at the party commented that the chair was such a thoughtful gift. I guess everyone except Mom."

I smiled when Regina told me what she overheard as her mother talked to some neighbors.

"Mom shrugged her shoulders and sighed as she told her friend, 'I don't know why they bought that expensive chair. Oh. I guess that it will be good for when I get old.'"

21

Finding a Permanent Solution

I worked in a dental office where most patients were seniors, and Agnes was one of our favorites. Agnes sustained an injury to her mouth and needed extensive dental work. Since she was living on a fixed income, the monetary restrictions made her choose the least expensive solution rather than the ideal option. The final product was a beautiful removable partial with porcelain teeth that were definitely more attractive than her natural teeth. Agnes was ecstatic with her new smile.

As sometimes happens, the clasp on her partial broke. She placed her dental appliance in a beautiful blue velvet box from an exclusive jewelry store.

Her husband, John, commented, "You know, Honey, that partial cost more than the necklace that came in that box." Agnes laughed and agreed.

On the way to the dentist, Agnes had to make one stop. While in church, someone stole the expensive-looking box from her unlocked car. Her partial was gone. Agnes was visibly upset and angry, but she did have a smirk on her face at the thought of the "jewel thief's" probable disappointment with his stolen treasure.

Sighing, Agnes realized she now had to have a new appliance made involving more impressions and, of course, more money. So, once again, she came in to pick up her new partial, vowing to be more careful.

A few days later, luck ran out yet again for Agnes. For some unknown reason, she took her partial out of her mouth after the church service and placed it in her coat pocket. When she arrived home, she planned to rinse it and insert it back in her mouth. Agnes placed her hand in her pocket to retrieve the partial and realized instead, she was putting her fingers into an empty hole in the lining. A sinking feeling came over her.

Panicked, she checked her purse and car and then, returning to the church parking lot retraced her steps. She hurried to the spot where she saw a glimmer in the sun. Agnes immediately spotted her partial on the pavement. Her excitement soon faded as she discovered a vehicle had run over her precious partial. It was squashed flat as a pancake!

Having to call for another round of whirlwind appointments to make another new partial was embarrassing. Agnes was mortified. Dr. Richards just shook his head in disbelief and took new impressions.

Bad luck for Agnes continued; this time, a tooth broke on the partial. She was afraid to tell her husband that having this cheaper option of a partial denture was not working. She had the partial wrapped in a Kleenex in her purse. Again, Agnes was at church. When they passed the collection plate, she dug in her handbag for her offering, and somehow the Kleenex stuck to the envelope flap.

Before she realized the problem, the envelope with the partial attached went into the collection plate, and it made its way through the congregation. Agnes was too embarrassed to claim the false teeth and refused to go to "lost and found," even though the alternative consequence was gathering the courage to tell her husband she needed another new partial.

Dr. Richards explained, "Some people are just not meant to have a removable appliance. Before I make partial number four, maybe you should consider a fixed dental bridge that is bonded to existing teeth. Agnes couldn't lose it."

John rationalized, "I wish we had made this decision in the first place because these lost partials are costing a fortune."

The day Agnes's appliance was permanently cemented in her mouth, she showed us a fantastic smile. Dr. Richards was delighted to have a fun story to share with his patients. Agnes's husband, John, was the happiest of all because it was the end to pricey dental bills.

22

Bucking Bronco

Dr. Richards was an excellent dentist, but his office equipment was antiquated. Since dental chairs are incredibly pricey, Dr. Richards purchased a pre-owned treatment chair for hygienists. It was state-of-the-art compared to the outdated one that presently occupied the space.

As a hygienist, I was thrilled with his choice. The current chair didn't recline, forcing me to stand long hours and endure backbreaking positions. It was the 1980s before dental professionals could sit while working behind modern chairs.

Since most of our patients were senior citizens, we thought introducing a reclining chair would be problematic. Expecting more resistance, we were pleasantly surprised. Patients enjoyed the new relaxation that came with reclining.

About a week after the new, gently used chair's installation, Mrs. Sweet, an elderly patient with an attitude much younger than her years, arrived for her appointment. She was a remarkable woman and somewhat of a celebrity in our town. Mrs. Sweet worked until she was ninety-seven, holding the same position at the same Fanny Farmer candy store for over sixty years. Everyone knew her, especially since her name was synonymous with sumptuous chocolate confections.

She purchased a bright red Mustang convertible to treat herself to a retirement gift. Mrs. Sweet loved driving with the top down, proudly waving to everyone, and she was still driving the beautiful car even though she was approaching her hundredth birthday. Local journalists were writing newspaper articles about her exciting life, career, and of course, her hot red car.

When she arrived for her dental appointment, Mrs. Sweet was delighted that we had framed the recent newspaper article featuring a picture of her seated in her beloved convertible posing in front of the candy store.

Unfortunately, we learned that a recent fire had just destroyed her home and her precious car. She was devastated. The blaze also precipitated her moving into assisted living. She stared at the photo and said, "My wild car kept me young; now life is boring and dull."

Knowing we had to keep on schedule, I guided her to the new chair, showed her how she needed to sit, and then leaned back until she felt comfortable in the chair. I explained that I would slowly put her in a reclining position. I quickly added, "Mrs. Sweet, if you're uncomfortable, I promise I'll reposition the chair." All went well with her appointment until it was time for Mrs. Sweet to leave my treatment room.

I pushed the upright button to return the chair to its original, factory-set vertical position. Immediately, it became unmistakable that something was amiss. The installation technician had crossed some wires allowing them to rub raw, creating a short. This malfunction caused the chair to groan, then jolt the back of the chair forward, and in the next movement, it collapsed to a full recline. The propulsion continued in a rhythmic bucking motion that nearly catapulted Mrs. Sweet from the room. As the jerking persisted, she tightly grasped the arms of the chair. To our surprise and amazement, Mrs. Sweet wasn't screaming but whooping and hollering like a rodeo star.

Everyone came running to see what was causing the horrendous banging. Nothing worked to stop the action, even cutting the power switch. Finally, Dr. Richards ran to the closet that held the mechanics, opened the electrical panel, and flipped the breaker. It seemed like an eternity, but it was actually only a matter of minutes before the madness ceased.

We were in a panic, but Mrs. Sweet giggled with delight. She said it reminded her of watching rodeo kings riding a bucking bronco. "I felt all that was missing today was a cowboy hat in my hand," she exclaimed.

"Who would guess Mrs. Sweet would find this enjoyable?" I sighed in relief.

She uttered, "Now that I no longer have my sporty car, nothing this exciting has happened since I moved to the HOME."

Dr. Richards was extremely grateful that Mrs. Sweet was unharmed. We all apologized profusely. Dr. Richards told her, "Mrs. Sweet, I assure you we are getting rid of this chair and only purchasing new, factory-delivered equipment."

In an excited voice, Mrs. Sweet said, "Really, Dr. Richards?"

She was smirking as she teasingly said, "Is there any chance you could have this thing delivered to my new home? It's like the amusement ride I put quarters in when I was a kid. The residents would love it!"

Mrs. Sweet continued to be an excellent patient until the magnificent age of one hundred and two. Then, the Good Lord called her home, appropriately, on the sweetest day of the year, Valentine's Day.

23

An Arrested Development

I hated working on Saturday. It seemed weekends brought out the worst in some patients. To make matters worse, it was the first beautiful, spring-like day after a particularly snowy winter, and my boss, Dr. Richards, was antsy. He was ready to leave, but I still had one more patient to see.

Since the man in my dental chair had been a patient for a few years, Dr. Richards checked him and instructed me to apologize to the last patient. Then, he headed out, leaving me alone for the rest of the afternoon.

I was cleaning George's teeth when I heard the office door open. Since no one was due for quite a while, I excused myself to see who was in the waiting room. I was surprised to see two police officers.

First, an extremely tall officer asked me if George was a patient. I replied, "Yes." Next, he said, "We went to his house, and his wife told us he was at his dental appointment. Is George here now?"

I had no idea what to say, so I nervously nodded in acknowledgment. So, question three was, "Is he finished with his treatment?"

My big mistake was to say "No." The officer looked at my panicked expression and said, "Ma'am, just finish with what you were doing. We'll wait right here."

I hesitated. *What am I to do?* I thought. I know George heard the entire conversation. My mind was racing. I rationalized; *the police would never have sent me back in there if he was dangerous. Would they?* I was hoping I was correct.

The silence was deafening upon re-entering the treatment room; all I could think about was that tray of sharp instruments within George's reach. I thought about the back door behind me that I could use as my escape route.

I finished George's cleaning in record time. Now it was apparent George was stalling. He suddenly became chatty and delayed getting out of the dental chair. I tried to keep my manner calm. "George, I have to prepare the room for my next patient. I'll send you a bill. Bye." My heart was thumping so loudly I was sure George could hear it.

Finally, he left the room, and I stayed behind. I heard the police officer tell George he had to come with them. They promptly escorted him out of the office.

Moments later, Jane, my next patient, entered the building. She ran into our office, understandably upset. She blurted out. "Oh, my gosh, two police officers just handcuffed a man in the foyer."

I was shivering. "The police just took that man out of my chair! Can you imagine?"

Trying to relieve the tension, I told Jane that as I secretly planned my escape, all I could picture was me wielding my tiny mouth mirror as a weapon in Kung Fu moves. We both chuckled. Carefully, I locked up the office with Jane and me inside. Somehow, I was able to compose myself and clean Jane's teeth.

Before I left for the day, I called Dr. Richards. I told him I wanted character references the next time he left me alone with a patient. Being a practical joker, Dr. Richards thought I was making up the story, but after listening to the shaky tone in my voice, he realized I was on the level.

It wasn't until I was on my way home that the gravity of the situation hit me. I realized that I should have never gone back into that room, and the officers put me at risk by insisting I finish. If George had panicked, this story would have had a different ending.

We never did find out why the police arrested George, nor did he ever return as a patient. However, you can be sure that Dr. Richards never left any staff member at the office alone ever again.

Having a patient arrested right out of my chair was a first for me. I could hardly wait to see what excitement the following Saturday would bring.

24

Hooking the Big One

I've had some of the most bizarre and unpredictable things happen in our dental office on Saturdays. Of course, patients loved the convenience of weekend hours, but the strange events, occurring only on this particular day of the week, made me wonder if having the office open was such a good idea.

I was at the front desk when two young boys charged through the door. All I could muster in a weak voice was, "Dr. Richards, we need you upfront immediately."

"We need to see the doctor right now. Please help us." They shouted in unison.

Both boys were now crying, and Dr. Richards' eyes widened as he peered into the disfigured face that stood before us.

I explained, "You're in a dental office. I don't think we can help you."

"Pleeeease!" the younger brother pleaded. Dr. Richards took one look at the older boy's face and knew I was correct.

The blonde-haired teenager was about sixteen. A sizeable rusty fishhook with a beautiful fly attached pierced his cheek near his lower lip. Making the matter worse, the boys had tried to get the hook out themselves. We saw the barb puncturing the soft tissue, tearing it to shreds. He was going to need plastic surgery. His face was a mess.

The injured boy attempted to speak. He said, "I was teaching my brother to fly fish in the creek behind this building."

The younger brother interrupted, sobbing, "Mom's going to kill me. I'm so sorry. I'm so sorry."

I reassured them. "Boys, everything is going to be fine. Dr. Richards, do you want me to call 911?" I thought *good thing they knew enough to cut the line so the weight of the pole didn't do any more damage.*

Calmly, Dr. Richards said, "You boys need an emergency room. How about if we call your mom? You can wait here until she comes."

Twenty minutes later, a hysterical mom ran into the office carrying a toddler. Horrified by the sight of her son's face, the woman immediately turned pale and keeled over. Evidently, she wasn't good at the sight of blood. The toddler in her arms hit his head as they tumbled to the floor. It was utter chaos! The toddler was screaming, and the boys were shrieking. The mom lay still.

Dr. Richards knelt near the woman while I got out the smelling salts. The younger brother grabbed the toddler. The pungent odor brought the mom around when I broke open the capsule and held it under her nose. Fortunately, the waiting room was empty.

The mom felt too shaky to drive, so she called her husband. We had difficulty keeping everyone calm while waiting for the boy's dad. It was a relief when he arrived.

"Maybe we should have just called 911," I said to Dr. Richards, stifling a laugh. "That's a great story. I know you'll find a way to tell your patients."

To show her gratitude, the boy's mom stopped by the office a week later with a tray of cookies. She reported her son had surgery, and his face looked great.

She apologized, saying, "So sorry we caused such a commotion that day."

I told her, "I was glad we could help."

As she left, she turned her head and said, "By the way, my boys now brag about the day they hooked the "big one."

25

What In the World Is a Key Fob?

I admired Samantha's new car as I watched her pull into the parking lot for her dental appointment. While I was seating her in my dental chair, I thought *she always has a story. I better get started before she starts talking.*

Oops, too late, Samantha started babbling. She described the trials and tribulations she experienced since she picked up her new car three months ago. She had me laughing from the start, so I had to stop and listen.

"The salesman handed me this electronic device and expected me to know what to do with it," Samantha snickered.

In such a matter-of-fact manner, he said, "Here's your key fob."

I asked. "What in the world is a key fob? In the good old days, you had two keys. One opened the doors; the other you inserted into the ignition. I can never remember if you turned it clockwise or counterclockwise, but you just knew how to bring the engine to life."

Samantha continued, "Nowadays, I have a gadget that if I merely walk by the car, the doors will unlock. Also, I can remotely start the engine or push a button initiating a screeching panic warning everyone ignores."

I nodded.

From past experiences, I observed Samantha always took forever to make a decision. The determining factor in her choice of the cherry red Chrysler sedan was the salesman's guarantee that you can't possibly ever lock your keys in the car.

"Wonderful," she remarked. "I have a tendency to slam the door before I check if I have the keys."

"Leave it to me." Samantha chuckled. "The very first day I had the car, I proved the salesman wrong,"

I started, "How could you possibly manage to …"

Samantha quickly interrupted. "I grabbed my gym bag from the trunk. A moment too late, I noticed my keys on the trunk mat just as I slammed it shut. I began to panic but then remembered the salesman's exact words."

She was grinning from ear to ear. "I guess the car dealer didn't know you could lock your keys in the trunk. My husband came to the rescue with the spare key."

"I bet he wasn't too happy," I snickered.

"Oh wait, it gets better," Samantha laughed.

"The next week, I went to the mall. I approached my car, and nothing happened. The door was supposed to unlock automatically. It wouldn't open, so I pressed the button on the device, but still, no response. I figured the battery was dead."

"I thought those things lasted forever," I commented. "I have one and never had a problem."

"Well, I fiddled with it but had no luck, so I had to call my husband for the second time to rescue me with this key thingy."

"Hmm," I giggled.

Samantha grinned, "I realized just before my husband pulled in that I was at the wrong car. It was too late. I took quite a razzing."

"You've got to be kidding," I remarked.

"Nope, that was only the second problem with this gadget. There's more." Samantha said, "Do you remember that freak morning snow a few weeks ago?"

I was about to speak, but she wasn't waiting for an answer.

"I left the gym and was astonished to find three inches of powdery snow covering my car. Using my key fob, I chirped the door open. Quickly, I grabbed the snow brush and meticulously cleaned every flake from the entire vehicle. Then just as I was going to get in, I glanced at the back seat. I gasped. Oh, my gosh! I was staring at a child's booster seat. How could I have the wrong car again?"

"What are you talking about?" I asked.

"Evidently, both keys were on the same frequency. I looked around and found my red vehicle a few spaces over. I drove away just as I saw a lady with a toddler heading towards the car I had just brushed off. She was looking around the parking lot, trying to figure out who made the kind gesture."

"How embarrassing, but I think she would have understood," I murmured.

After listening to her story, I was able to finish Samantha's cleaning. As she was leaving, she commented, "I'm certainly not having good luck with this sophisticated technology."

"It appears not, my dear," I said with a smile.

Watching her in the parking lot, I thought *what are the odds an identical red sedan was parked right next to hers?*

I could see she wasn't paying attention as she pressed the key fob. Lights flashed, but that wasn't the car she was approaching. Instead, when she flung the door open, a man was asleep in the driver's seat. They both jumped and he let out an astonished screech.

As she apologized to the startled man, who was waiting for his wife, she looked up to see me peeking out my window. Red-faced, she rolled her eyes and shrugged her shoulders as she hurried to her car, laughing all the way.

26

Disappearing Car Caper

When my former co-worker, Regina, pulled up to the office, I was surprised that she wasn't driving the flashy red sports car I knew she had just purchased.

"Where's that retirement gift? I was hoping to see it." I exclaimed.

"It turns out the joy of my sports car was short-lived," Regina said, "I knew the Grand Opening of the new mall would be a madhouse, but I wanted in on the huge doorbuster sales."

She told me that after endlessly driving around, she finally found a parking space. "I wish I had used the valet parking. At the time, it seemed ridiculous to pay someone to park my car and wait for them to fetch it, but in hindsight, it would have been worth every penny."

Regina got settled in the dental chair and told me the story.

She said, "I heard developers intentionally designed this mall to make the customer get lost so they would wander around and spend more money."

"You know, I heard that too." With this information in mind, I planned ahead and carefully made myself aware of the exact entrance I came in and the number of the row in which I parked."

Regina continued her story. "I spent hours in the mall shopping. Exhausted, I trudged to the Macy's exit, arms laden with packages. I pulled out my keys, ready to press the button to unlock the car, but there was no little red sports car in row W."

She stated, "I know I entered Macy's entrance near the men's department. I'm sure I remember correctly. I parked in row W near the end."

It was a sweltering and humid day as Regina wandered the parking lot, trying to figure out what to do. Finally, she regrouped, went inside, and had a cold drink. Then, after studying the directory of stores on a map nearby, she exclaimed. "No wonder I can't find my car. Macy's is the anchor store with two locations, one at each end of the mall."

Overjoyed that she had solved the problem, Regina trekked to the other Macy's store. Sure enough, it had a similar men's department with a door entering from the outside. "I must have parked my car here," she thought. Regina arrived at the parking lot and found row WW. She realized the row marker read W in the other lot. "It is easy to get confused in this place," she muttered.

Confidently, Regina strolled down the row pressing her key fob and listening for the familiar chirp. Again, there wasn't a cute little red sports car anywhere in row WW or any other row nearby. "Am I going crazy? Wow, this was such a bad idea coming to the mall today," she said tearfully.

Regina was exasperated. She dared not call her husband and get the "I told you so" snide remark. Frustrated, she whimpered, "What am I going to do?" She wandered around aimlessly for quite a while and decided to reenter the mall.

Regina retraced her steps and even went back to look in row W again. "Am I completely losing my mind?" she fretted as she tried to find humor in the situation.

Unfortunately, it was getting late, and the mall was about to close. Ultimately, Regina had no choice but to go to the security office and ask for help. As she entered, she felt embarrassed and very foolish.

"Can I help, Ma'am?" The uniformed guard asked.

In a frustrated manner, Regina admitted, "I'm afraid I can't find my car."

"Where did you park it?" he asked.

"If I knew that answer, I wouldn't be here right now!" She said, holding back the tears.

Seeing how upset she was, the guards answered in a sympathetic tone, "Well, tell me your name and license plate number. I'll see what I can do." He smiled when she gave the information. "Didn't you hear us page you in the mall? For the last two hours, we announced for you to come to the security office every fifteen minutes."

Regina was perplexed, "What are you talking about?"

He began, "You see, earlier this evening, there was an accident in the parking lot involving your car."

Puzzled, Regina asked, "How could there be an accident? I wasn't in my car."

The guard said, "Yes, ma'am, that's what I am trying to explain. An elderly gentleman was parked nose to nose with your car. He put his huge SUV in drive instead of reverse and gave it a good amount of gas. His car practically climbed over your little car. The police came and towed both cars away."

With a cheerful tone, Regina said, "What a relief!"

Now, it was the guard's turn to look confused.

"I thought I was going crazy," she told the officer. "I was beginning to wonder if I even drove a car to the mall. I'll call home to ask my husband for a ride."

Her husband answered in a panicked voice, "Where in the world are you? The Sherriff was here looking for you."

When Regina heard her husband's voice, all she could blurt out was, "Oh, never mind that...Please just come pick me up!"

27

Miracle on the St. Lawrence River

Summer was fast approaching. Dr. Richards, my boss, mentioned that he and his son-in-law planned to build a guest cottage on their property in the Thousand Islands region of New York State.

He told me, "It's going to be a five-year project. We're starting with the pier foundation this summer."

I just looked at him and said, "My husband, Harry, could build the entire cabin for you in a weekend."

My boss raised his eyebrows, exclaiming, "Really? Are you sure?"

"My husband comes from a long line of accomplished carpenters. His father and his uncles owned a lumber yard specializing in custom millwork. Harry started working in the mill at the young age of seven. As he got older, skilled German craftsmen taught him the fine art of carpentry."

The planning began. Dr. Richards, his wife, Harry, and I went to dinner. The project started to take shape. Dr. Richards roughly sketched a simple cabin on a cocktail napkin at the restaurant. It was 1980, and this small town didn't require a building permit or fancy architectural drawings. Remarkably, the teeny napkin was the only set of plans.

Harry drew up a material list while Dr. Richards and his son-in-law completed the foundation works to cure the concrete before the framing began. Lumber, siding, roofing, paneling, and insulation were all delivered. As agreed, our entourage would arrive a few hours later. It was Thursday evening of a long four-day Memorial Weekend.

Morristown, New York, is a postage-stamp-sized town on the St. Lawrence River. It's a place where everyone knows each other. Back then, the local lumber yard carried inventory, providing everything needed, even for a project of this proportion.

Harry expressed concern, "It's the holiday weekend. Businesses will be closed. I hear the townspeople would rather enjoy the firemen's carnival than keep their shops open."

Dr. Richards assured Harry, "We're all set. The owner of the store gave me the key. He told me if we needed anything, we were to leave a list of the materials we took. Can you imagine?"

Our expert crew was raring to go as the sun peeked over the horizon. At dawn, Friday morning, Harry laid out the first studs of the exterior walls. Dr. Richards notified all the neighbors that there would be activity and noise from sun up to sundown.

The skill saws revved up and roared in the morning stillness. Like a finely tuned machine, the crew worked stick-building the cottage. Walls went up in record time. By that evening, all the walls were standing. The carpenters were already cutting rafters and preparing for installation on day two.

At dawn, the rafters were lifted and nailed. Next, part of the crew installed the plywood sheeting, followed by felt and roofing shingles. Then, closer to the ground, the remaining workers fitted windows and mounted siding.

Any builder will tell you extra lumber, nails, or screws may run short, and a trip to the lumber yard becomes necessary. It was a good thing the key to the lumber yard was available because they needed more framing lumber. After entering the padlocked area, loading the truck, and leaving a list on the counter, our errand boys should have remembered to secure the load properly.

As the truck turned the first corner the load shifted, strewing lumber over the road. The men were panicked when two police officers on patrol stopped them. The officers smiled, began reloading the planks, and remarked on the weekend project talked about all around town.

One officer said, "I've been anchored off the point all weekend. You guys are amazing. In a small town like this, it usually takes years to complete an undertaking of this magnitude."

His partner added, "The town's people are buzzing. No one had ever seen the likes of such a phenomenon."

The cabin was on a point jutting into the river. A constant parade of boats went by to observe the remarkable progress. By the second day, watercraft of all sizes dropped anchors, making it appear a small marina was present. Our crew hoisted an American flag to the highest peak with the exterior walls completed. Boat horns blasted. People cheered and applauded.

As promised over dinner and sketched out on a cocktail napkin, the cabin was framed, roofed, and sided over the four-day weekend, closing it in from the elements.

Looking pleased, Dr. Richards said, "You were right! If the rain had held, Harry could have completed the project."

I said, "If you give me next Saturday off, we'll return and finish."

"It's a deal!" he said, pumping his fist in the air.

We returned the following weekend. Part of the crew installed the flooring inside, while the others concentrated on building a wraparound deck. When we left, the cottage was move-in ready.

My boss was amazed, "Harry blew me away! Fifteen hundred square feet was a huge undertaking for five men in four days." He said with delight, "The locals are calling it *'the Miracle on the St. Lawrence.'*"

A collage of photos and the framed cocktail napkin hang in the office. The rough architectural drawing amuses countless patients. Dr. Richards has bragging rights that his camp, erected in record time, will forever be the talk of the little town, and today, forty years later, it still is.

28

Hitting the Waves

Dr. Richards' camp is located where the St Lawrence River is less than a mile wide, dividing the United States and Canada. It's part of the Seaway Project, which connects the Great Lakes with the Atlantic Ocean. Freighters of all shapes and sizes pass in the deep channel on the Canadian side of the river.

While my husband and crew built the guest cabin, Dr. Richards invited my father and me for a boat ride. "Why don't you and your dad take a break? You can take pictures of the construction's progress with a view from the water."

His smirk should have been a red flag. From firsthand experience, I knew he was the King of Practical Jokes. I was wrong to assume he was too busy to dream up anything and should have realized my boss was waiting for the right opportunity to spring his prank. Little did I know I was to be the intended recipient!

Not wanting to slow building progress or cut off his nose to spite his face, he didn't dare mess with Harry and the crew. That only left one person, me. The three of us donned our life jackets and boarded a small sixteen-foot motorboat. Dr. Richards headed straight for the freighters. I was terrified and gulped as I asked, "Do we need to be so close to that huge ship?" Ignoring me, he pulled our tiny craft alongside.

I noticed the cargo ship was producing a tsunami-like wake. Before I could complain, I spotted a mischievous expression in the boss's eyes. Dickie (his preferred nickname) gunned the engine of our tiny boat. Noticing the playful grin on his face, we were positive he had done this before with other passengers.

We flew over the waves crashing hard into the swells. Jostling and bouncing us in our seats, Dickie intended to toss me from my perch, but his plan backfired. My seventy-year-old father went airborne, landing on the floor of the boat. Dickie was apologetic because my poor dad was severely bruised and unable to return to his seat without assistance. It was amazing that he was not seriously injured. I think that was the real "Miracle on the St. Lawrence" that weekend.

Remorseful and apologizing profusely to my dad, Dickie said, "I'm really sorry, Joe, but just think of the great story you can tell." What he meant was, "Yeah, now I have another adventure to share with my patients."

At the office, he reiterated, "Joe, who served in the 82nd Airborne Unit during WWII, went airborne in my boat on the St Lawrence River. Unfortunately, I hit the wrong target. I was trying to throw Terry in the river." Dickie is always delighted to share his version of the airborne anecdote.

Now, it's my turn to tell the rest of the story. As usual, Dickie neglected to add some essential details when retelling the airborne story. Once he left the shipping channel, the sun's glare made traversing the shallower water difficult. At the helm, Dickie cautiously navigated, yet we hit a large shoal, which sheared a blade from the prop.

We lurched violently in a forward direction, and the impact almost threw us from the boat. A strong current was quickly sweeping our disabled craft downriver.

A master at storytelling, Dickie prefers to eliminate mention of the Mayday Call, to his wife, with a plea to rescue us with his other boat to tow us back to his dock. Also absent from the account is the mention of an enormous repair bill for a new propeller.

Mrs. Richards said, "It serves you right for injuring poor Joe. You can add this damaged propeller to the rest of your sizeable collection of, as the grandkids have coined them, Dickie's Blooper's."

I laughed as she told me, "The main cabin features a wall dedicated to the numerous broken propellers." I observed a sizeable square bronze plaque prominently displayed on the wall. "I had it engraved in huge bold letters." She said. "The sentiment is simple. It reads 'Dickie's Wall of Shame.'"

Dozens of mounted damaged props take up an entire wall. I used my wide-angle lens to take a snapshot. After getting the evidence on film, a close-up of the plaque seemed appropriate. With the help of Photoshop and some creative editing, I added Dickie to the photo. I now had a masterpiece. My revenge is the eleven by fourteen framed image of the boss standing before his "Wall of Shame."

29

The Queen's Wave

Lynn was settling into the dental chair, telling me that she and her sister, Janet, had just returned from Iceland. Since Janet's appointment was next, she joined us in the treatment room so I could get the whole story. Lynn said, "Things never go smoothly, and I have another unique travel story. I think these kinds of things only happen to us."

She began her story, "I had difficulty adjusting to the twenty hours of daylight, and my tummy was annoyingly sensitive. Tired of staying close to my hotel room, I decided to gulp some Pepto-Bismol and grab my guidebook."

Janet said, "I was sympathetic to my sister's plight, so I Googled *toilets in Iceland*. I told Lynn the website boasted of clean, modern, self-cleaning restrooms."

Lynn was comforted to learn they were numerous on street corners throughout the city. Janet turned the computer screen towards Lynn and showed her a futuristic-looking round building that housed the state-of-the-art comfort facility. The webpage gave a handy tip: most restrooms charged a few coins to open the door.

They left the hotel and joined the ninety-minute walking tour of Reykjavik they had booked before they left home. It was exciting seeing so many sights in this beautiful city.

"It wasn't long before I felt a foreboding. There was a distinct rumbling in my gut." Lynn said in a troubled voice. "Just as I feared, a sudden urgency overpowered me. Frantically, I looked around, and my pace became a trot as I rushed to the corner."

Lynn explained, "I fumbled with the correct coins and dashed inside. Hurriedly I pulled down my pants as the door slowly closed. I plopped my purse and camera in the sink. Thankfully, I found some relief, but my stomach kept cramping. I moaned as the sweat poured off my forehead. The spasms had me buckling over. I was sorry I told Janet to have the tour group wait."

As promised, the restroom was immaculate. It was a private single room with a toilet and a sink. The pristine white walls contrasted with the polished stainless steel fixtures. A curved motorized door opened directly to the street.

Lynn continued, "I was in extreme discomfort, and I accidentally hit the flush mechanism, which initiated a series of events. First, the self-cleaning feature of the restroom automatically turned on the sink that housed my purse and camera, immediately drenching my belongings. Next, I heard a mechanical grinding whirling sound, and the door started to open.

Lynn said, "I was living my worst nightmare. I cried out loud. No, no, no, noooooooooo..."

Lynn still had her pants dangling down around her ankles when, to her horror, daylight started pouring into the building.

"What can I do? What can I possibly do?" The horrid realization of what was happening overwhelmed her. She was there for all of Reykjavik to see. She cringed and couldn't move.

Beet red, Lynn sat looking mortified. She pleaded, "Janet, make them leave! Our tour group is staring at me." She was whimpering loudly as the door continued to open wider.

"My head hung low. When I looked up, I gave a weak, embarrassed smile. Then suddenly, the absurdity of the situation overtook me. I started to mimic a movement, open-palmed with a twist of my wrist, known as the 'Queen's Royal Wave.' I decided I might as well make the best of this since I couldn't make it disappear." She thought, "This would actually be funny if it weren't happening to me."

"Perched on the *throne,* I just raised my head, grinned, and self-consciously continued waving. I groaned and waved, groaned and waved, until mercifully, the door timed out. It eventually closed ever so slowly; for me, it was an eternity!"

The onlookers expressed empathy for the poor tourist. Fortunately, the crowds dispersed, and Janet doubled over in bouts of laughter.

Lynn scowled at her sister as she exited the glorified outhouse. Janet exclaimed, "Lynn, you looked somewhat regal, waving to the crowds!"

"Let's get out of here!" Lynn cried.

Relieved to be back at their hotel, Lynn spent the rest of the afternoon snuggled in the comfy bed, trying to forget the embarrassing incident. She was starting to doze when a news report on the TV caught her attention. The announcer was talking over the video of the brand-new traffic cams that had just gone into operation the day before.

The camera showed cars going by precisely the same corner where the fiasco occurred. The restroom was in plain sight, and you could see the door opening. Lynn squealed as the news anchor said, "Folks, this report has a bizarre twist. It seems…"

Lynn pleaded with Janet to turn up the volume. "What did he say? Oh, my gosh!" she shrieked.

Janet said, "I clicked off the TV. So we'll never know if Lynn was the star of the evening news."

30

Moulin Rouge

My boss, Dr. Richards, Dickie, as we call him, enjoyed staying in one place while his wife, Julie, loved to travel. So when they became empty nesters, they came up with a great idea. Dickie made Julie happy by financing a trip of her choice and taking along office personnel as travel companions while he got to stay home. It proved the best of both worlds. Naturally, we were thrilled to be a part of these adventures.

We were surprised when they explained this unexpected, generous office incentive award that began in 1996. Dickie gave Julie his credit card, and we made sure his American Express saw lots of action all over the world. Julie had a favorite saying, "If you want it, buy it!" She certainly did abide by her mantra without any guilt holding her back.

In 2003, we arrived at Dr. Richards' house for brunch, and Monsignor Edwards, a personal friend of our boss, joined us.

Dr. Richards introduced his guest. "Monsignor has lived in France for the last fifteen years, and I am eager for him to show you some of his favorite places."

We didn't fully comprehend until we looked under our placemats and there were plane tickets to France.

Beginning in Paris, our all-expense paid itinerary incorporated a ten-day trip through France's wine country with major cities and prominent attractions. Even though we were on tour with a professional guide, Monsignor added his personal touch, sharing his impressive knowledge of French history and culture. Our marvelous trip was a dream come true.

We discussed how we could repay Monsignor for adding so much to our trip. We had an idea but kept our destination a secret. As the taxi stopped in front of the red building with a windmill on top, Monsignor looked a little startled as he was familiar with the historic landmark's reputation. Monsignor started to say, "Ladies, you do know that…"

Julie was so excited she interrupted, "Since we were returning to Paris, we thought it would be fun to treat you to dinner and a show at the internationally acclaimed Moulin Rouge, famous for the creation of the Can-Can."

Tickets were available for exclusive seating in a private balcony with an unobstructed view of the stage. Music blared, and dancers did high-kicking moves in choreographed precision, enchanting the audience. Sipping champagne and devouring our decadent French dinners, we toasted, as was our tradition. *Thank you Dickie! Ooh, La La! Magnifique!*

After intermission, more showgirls appeared on stage in elaborate costumes covered in rhinestones, sequins, and feathers. Beautiful dancers paraded Las Vegas style across the stage with large plumes covering their upper torsos. In unison, we exhaled audible gasps as the dancers spread their arms. We never read the tickets' fine print saying "adult entertainment."

Julie turned to me, "I knew Moulin Rouge had a first-class cabaret show advertised as providing an atmosphere of total euphoria. Now I know why!"

These four naïve Catholic women didn't know the rest of the show was topless. We noticed the Monsignor had raised his eyebrows, but he couldn't hide the huge smile on his face. Unintentionally, we treated a Monsignor, a Roman Catholic priest, as our guest, to a tasteful but nudie show.

You can be sure Dr. Richards got a lot of mileage from our faux pas, and in retrospect, we provided Monsignor Edwards with some colorful stories of his own to share.

31

Fancy Pants In France

You have heard the story of our incredible trip to France, but getting there was a totally different matter. It was 2003; the world was still reeling from the terrorist attack on 9/11. People were suspicious of air travel, especially international flights. We planned our dream trip of *April in Paris* long before the decimation of the towers. We weren't sure our fantasy would become a reality.

Further complicating matters was an outbreak of a highly contagious virus, SARS. Severe Acute Respiratory Syndrome was predominantly present in Asia but threatened to spread worldwide. In addition, we saw posted warnings that confined spaces during air travel posed a significant danger displayed throughout the airport. Even making matters worse, our city was amid a debilitating ice storm, and we had been without power for days. As a result, we seriously considered canceling our trip.

Our families thought we were insane, but we decided to make our planned trip, not realizing how difficult this task would become. However, we were seasoned travelers confident that our carry-on bag stocked with masks, gloves, and hand sanitizer would suffice to keep us safe.

Arriving at the airport, we found our scheduled flight canceled due to a snowstorm in our connecting city, Philadelphia. Unfortunately, this meant we would miss our plane overseas, but a helpful ticket agent found a flight from Rochester, NY, to Toronto, where we could transfer to a red-eye direct to Paris. Little did we know we were talking about a twelve-seater Cessna that would get bounced around in the storm.

The Rochester flight crew rushed us so we could depart before they closed the airport, but they assured us our bags were checked straight through to Paris and would be there when we landed.

In Canada, we attempted to find our next flight. The gate agent informed us that we should have picked up our bags, brought them through customs, rebooking them to Paris.

We looked at each other confused. I said, "No one told us we had to go through customs."

With a stern expression, the gate attendant said, "I'm not sure how you avoided customs, but I'll search the database to see what airline has your bags."

The airport was practically deserted, and we were running out of time. We had a choice, run to catch the flight with no baggage and hope our luggage would find us, or miss a day of our trip.

Figuring we could make do with just our carry-on, we sprinted to the gate for the flight to Paris, arriving out of breath. Now, sorry to say, they informed us we had not been in Canada long enough to board this flight. Unfortunately, none of our desperate pleas or explanations could convince the gate agent to let us board.

We were back to square one. We were a pitiful sight by then! After an extensive hunt, passing one closed kiosk after another, we were befriended by a sympathetic ticket agent who was closing up her station. She booked us on a flight arriving in Paris only twelve hours later than scheduled. The biggest glitch was she wasn't sure if they would let us board because we had no luggage. It was a typical *Catch Twenty-two*.

We had no way of notifying our travel agent of our dilemma and only hoped we could catch up with the tour before the bus departed Paris for another city. Hopeful, we waited to board this plane. Our careful pre-planning for premium aisle seats vanished, but at least we were allowed on the flight.

When we landed in Paris, we reported our missing luggage and prayed for the best.

We arrived at our hotel, looking somewhat bedraggled. Our tour operator, Genevieve, was in the lobby. She exclaimed, "Hooray, we've found our missing tourists! Everyone made the connection in Philly, and no one knew what happened to you. Monsignor was worried." She continued, "Our boat tour of the Seine is in thirty minutes."

Since we had no luggage and thus nothing to change into, we freshened up and were on our way to see France. We were about thirty-six hours without sleep, but that strong European coffee perked us up. Luckily, we had our coats and gloves. April in Paris can be very chilly.

Genevieve pointed us to a typical souvenir shop and a lingerie boutique to quickly secure our needed items. "There isn't much time," she warned. "Shop quickly,"

We each purchased two t-shirts at the souvenir shop. One would serve as a nightshirt, while the other would be a change of clothes for the morning. At the boutique, we weren't as fortunate. Nothing fit the criteria for our mature bodies.

It only carried designer lingerie; there were only two style choices, incredibly uncomfortable-looking thongs or undergarments covered with ruffles on the backside, resembling panties you put under baby girl's dresses. Settling on the ruffles, we were reminded of the childish ditty that mentions London, France, and underpants.

We had no choice; we did need clean undies. We coined these bloomers our "fancy pants in France" because the ruffles made our trousers balloon out, looking all poufy on our derrieres. In addition, their cumbersome design made us waddle, giving the appearance we were wearing adult diapers under our clothing. We laughed, "What a hoot! Wait until Dickie hears this one."

We rented bikes in Avignon. We laughed as we pictured ourselves on the *Tour de France* and were grateful those bloomers padded out seats as we road for miles.

Our ten days in France flew by in a flash. Each night delicious French wine splashed as our glasses clinked. Together, we toasted, "Thank you, Dickie. You are the best boss ever!"

32

Lost Luggage Flasco

We made it to France, but our suitcases were missing. We were seasoned travelers, but it was our first tour on a bus. The travel agency issued each vacationer a small carry-on tote with the company logo. Due to the limited-spaced in the baggage compartment under the bus, the tour company requested that we only bring the provided bag and one suitcase.

However, when we found the other thirty passengers on the bus brought multiple suitcases and larger carry-ons, we were sorry we obeyed the mandate. In unison, we commented, "If at least one of us had our suitcase, we could share some clothing."

Our families demanded that if we insisted on making this trip, we protect ourselves from this virus that threatened travelers. So instead of the items we usually packed, such as a change of clothes, undies, pajamas, and toiletries, we managed to fit only essential PPE (Personal Protection Equipment), latex gloves, hand sanitizer, and masks. We shoved everything into this little carry-on, and even with these limited items, it was difficult to zip.

Being from a dental office, at least we had our toothbrushes, but were we sorry that we had no changes of clothing. We quickly realized the underwear and two T-shirts we purchased the first night weren't enough. Since we changed hotels daily, our plan of washing out items wasn't working. Our clothing was still wet when our suitcases had to be loaded on the bus.

Fellow passengers were sympathetic, but after seeing us in the same attire for three days, they offered us perfume. We assured them we bathed, but somehow we had to devise a plan to secure some clothing.

Our tour guide, Genevieve, came to our rescue on the third night. With an armload of clothes, she appeared at our hotel room door. We were appreciative but skeptical because Genevieve had a relatively stocky build, and we doubted anything would fit.

"We still have no word about your suitcases, and with changing cities almost every night, the odds of them catching up with you is unlikely." But, she added excitedly, "I rummaged through my teenage daughter's closets to come up with some things you might be able to wear."

We threw the clothing on a bed, and our "fashion show" began. As a group of sixty-something tourists, we found that the choices from the daughter's closet were trendy and certainly not age-appropriate. I held up some items and chuckled, "It looks like slim pickings of anything we could hope to wear."

I tried to contain myself as we searched through the clothing. "What was Genevieve thinking?"

Dr. Richards' wife tried on a relatively tight t-shirt. When she pulled it over her head, we hooted at the two strategically placed prominent sequined stars that framed her ample bosom. The stars bounced and jiggled as she strutted around the hotel room, run-way style. Nothing was left to the imagination when the trimmings shimmered in the light, making her chest glow neon colors. Finally, we could no longer control ourselves, laughing until we cried.

After passing on a see-through blouse, I did find a gorgeous pink cashmere sweater that was comfy and warm. My companions were also able to salvage a few items. We felt better and thanked our tour guide the next day.

No word on the luggage as we approached day seven. Since we were staying two nights in Nice, we were delighted to hear the airline located the missing pieces and could deliver all four bags. We cheered, and our tour group applauded.

Our joy was short-lived. The bags, covered with various airport codes, arrived shrink-wrapped because they were severely damaged.

This hotel didn't have bellhops or elevators, and this was before suitcases had wheels. We dragged our overweight belongings up five flights of stairs.

After complaining for days about not having our clothes, I moaned, "It looks like our valises went on their own adventure. Do we truly want all this stuff now?"

To make matters worse, we were all in one tiny room with barely enough floor space to stand. I grumbled, "Where are we going to put these? "

In France that year, we learned a valuable lesson. We should have known the manufacturer's brand and the size and color of our luggage. It would have expedited their return.

The second lesson we learned was that less is better. Travel light is our new motto. The four of us managed just fine for almost ten days and realized we could have crammed a lot into something smaller that would have fit in the overhead compartment.

We made an important decision that day for our future travels; we would never check a piece of baggage again!

33

Stuck Again

I left work early because the snow had intensified, and patients were canceling appointments. The weatherman predicted that the worst was yet to come. Heading home, I was dreading the condition of my seven-hundred-foot-long driveway. It always drifted over, and I was constantly getting stuck. Even the kid's school bus driver would comment, "Your mom is stuck again!" My kids found it as embarrassing as I did.

I prayed all the way home, "Please, please, let my driveway be passable." I had to slow down to turn into the driveway, thus losing the momentum I needed to plow through the two-foot-deep snow drifts. Slamming my palms against the steering wheel, I screamed in frustration. "I knew it! Stuck again! Now, what am I going to do?"

I was trapped by the hard-packed snow banks on either side of the car. The car door wouldn't open. Escaping through the passenger door seemed a better option since the snow pile looked lower.

It was not an easy task in a bulky coat and boots, but I managed to crawl across the center console. Pushing with all my strength was futile because the door wouldn't budge. I groaned as I remembered that this door freezes shut in the sub-zero weather.

Again, I became a contortionist, wriggling over the console only to find myself back behind the steering wheel just where I started. "OK, Now what?" I said aloud.

It would have been an easy fix if cell phones were commonplace at the time. Car phones were a luxury, but now I wished I had purchased one despite the expense. I weighed my options and mumbled, "No one is due home for hours. I can't just sit here with the motor running because I don't know if the tailpipe is above the snow." Risking carbon-monoxide poisoning by staying warm with the engine ruining versus shutting down and freezing to death were not great options. So I needed to formulate a plan.

The power windows were unpredictable. Hoping the temperamental window on the driver's door worked, I prayed as I depressed the button. Miraculously, the window lowered, and I slipped out the window on my belly head-first into the snow. I righted myself and trudged in the knee-deep snow into the house.

The wind was howling, so I bundled up in long johns, a coat, hat, gloves, and warm snow boots. Then, with an unwavering determination, I grabbed a shovel. A sane person would have stayed in the comfort of the warm house, but I wanted to move that car into the garage if it was the last thing I ever did!

Like a maniac in a cartoon, I shoveled and shoveled. But, unfortunately, with the winds howling, more snow was landing in the car than clearing a path. I tried moving the car repeatedly, and I had to climb back through the driver's window each time. Positioning myself on the cold mound of snow on the driver's seat, I tried to nudge the car onward. My progress was inches, and I was frustrated because my driveway was so long.

"It's freezing out," I moaned. I couldn't take any more razzing about all the times I've been stuck in the snow this year alone, so I continued.

However, I stayed out there much longer than I realized, as now it was beginning to get dark. On the sixth try, I successfully moved the car more than a few inches. Finally, I had enough cleared snow to gun the gas pedal and plowed the car through the last hundred feet into the garage. "Hooray!" I shouted.

I parked the car, brushed the piles of snow from inside the car, and went into the warm house. My fingers and toes were throbbing as they thawed out. I brewed hot tea, sipping until my outsides and insides were warm.

As I sat down, my husband called to tell me he had just hired someone to plow the driveway. "A little late," I mumbled.

"What do you mean?" He asked. "You're not stuck in the middle of the driveway again, are you?"

"I am not! Oh, never mind," I replied, as I continued to sip my soothing tea with my frozen hands wrapped around that warm cup.

34

Slip Sliding Away

When my sixty-year-old coworker Pamela arrived at the office Monday morning, I asked, "Did you have any trouble getting home Friday? The roads were awful."

She told me the drive home from work was harrowing. "I've never been so disoriented driving in the snow. The storm caused whiteouts, zero visibility, and treacherous conditions. You'd think driving in the city, the buildings would diminish the blowing snow, but I found myself in a parking lot and had no idea how I got there."

I replied, "My drive home was a white-knuckle experience too. I thought you would wait out the storm."

"I waited a while but took a chance since I only live a few miles from work. When I arrived home, I was happy to see my husband parked on the street, leaving the driveway for me."

We had time before our patients arrived, so I listened to her story. I knew she had been cautious on the snow and ice since her knee surgery; the last thing she needed was to fall. She told me the weeks of continuous snow storms made snow banks about five feet high on each side of her driveway. "It's like driving into a tunnel," she joked.

"My driveway, too," I agreed as I packaged instruments for sterilization.

Pamela told me she started getting out of the car, but something stopped her. The blinding snow had let up, and the sun was shimmering off the packed snow giving the driveway an icy look. Gingerly, she put her foot out of the car; sure enough, it was a sheet of ice. She hesitated because she knew it was too slippery to get out. Pamela dug in her purse for her cell phone and sighed as she remembered putting it down to put her boots on, and she was sure it was still at the office. She needed a plan to get in the house.

Her husband couldn't hear Pamela repeatedly honking the car horn from the family room in the back of the house. Her dog was alerted, barking incessantly, but that didn't bring her husband to the window either. Pamela was beyond frustrated. She tried moving the car, only to have the tires spin on the ice, not getting any traction. Finally, she thought, "It's time to execute. Plan B once I form one."

Pamela grabbed her snow brush that had a telescoping handle. She extended the brush and reached out, trying to pull fresh snow from the banks to cover the ice. It took her quite a while to lay a new base of snow. She was successful, or so she thought.

She repositioned herself in the driver's seat, turning her body so her feet hung out the door. Again, she carefully placed one foot and then the other on the ground while holding on to the steering wheel and door frame. Slowly, she stood, and her feet went out from under her at that exact moment. She was still holding onto the door and steering wheel as she fell backward into the car, hitting her head on the center console. She landed in a supine position with her feet dangling straight out the door, not touching the ground. She couldn't move.

Pamela wished she had put the seat back, giving herself extra room when she tried to get out because now she was wedged between it and the steering wheel. The absurdity of her ridiculous predicament, pinned with her head hanging over the console on the passenger side, caused her to giggle.

She told me, "I thought maybe if I flap my feet, I can position myself differently, but my boots felt like twenty-pound weights as I was flailing, trying to squirm and wriggle free. My arms were useless, trapped at my sides, ruling out grabbing the steering wheel for leverage."

I listened as Pamela told me she gave one final effort. "I squirmed and twisted and wiggled until I turned just enough to dislodge myself and right myself behind the steering wheel."

Unfortunately, the short-lived victory turned to exasperation since she saw no solution to her predicament.

Exhausted and freezing, Pamela attempted to signal her husband again by blowing the horn. Her dog was in the front window barking and jumping up and down, but there was no sign of her husband. Pamela began to cry. "Just as I thought I was going to freeze to death in my driveway, my husband came out to rescue me."

He said, "Mrs. Jones, next door, called and said you looked like you needed some help. She was laughing so hard I had a hard time understanding her."

Pamela sighed, "Once we were inside and I warmed up, my husband explained what Mrs. Jones told him. She said the snow had kept her housebound for weeks, and this was the funniest thing she'd seen in a long time. The sight out her front window was mesmerizing, but she began feeling guilty watching. Finally, she picked up the phone."

Smiling, Pamela added, "At that point, I forgave my neighbor; I was so relieved to be safe and warm that I was crying and laughing at the same time."

35

Nut or Lug Nut

Sam, one of my favorite patients, rushed into the office, apologizing for being late. He was flustered, wheezing, and pale. I suggested we reschedule the appointment. Sam explained, "I've been out in the cold, which triggered my asthma, but I hated to cancel on short notice."

After reading his blood pressure which was extremely high, and assessing his general condition for a man in his seventies, we agreed to reappoint. He confided in me the morning had been disastrous, but I needed to keep this to myself if he continued. So, knowing the calming effect some therapeutic listening could do, I sat and paid attention.

"Early this morning, my grandson, Kevin, called with a frantic, panicky voice. He was on his way to school when his car hit construction debris on the road. He had a flat tire."

Sam told me that Kevin had studied all week for an important physics exam, and now he desperately needed a ride so he wasn't late. Kevin pleaded, "Grandpa, I also need help fixing the tire."

"On my way to pick up Kevin, a huge deer darted out from behind a barn, just inches from my vehicle, causing me to swerve. I skidded, coming to a dead stop, narrowly missing driving into a ravine. Just as I breathed a sigh of relief, an entire herd bolted into the open, leaping over the hood of my car one after another."

"That must have been terrifying," I commented.

Sam continued, "It was a miracle! There wasn't a scratch on either the car or the deer."

Sam said he pulled up, and his grandson was pacing impatiently beside his disabled vehicle. The predicted storm had started dumping huge flakes of heavy wet snow. Recounting the deer story, Sam began driving Kevin to his exam.

"Boy, we're both having quite a morning!" Kevin said.

Sam wished his grandson luck on this exam and said he would wait in the nearby coffee shop until the test was over. Besides, he could use some time out of the car.

Kevin completed his exam, and the pair returned to the section of the road where they abandoned the SUV. They were grateful it was still there, and the police hadn't towed it. Unfortunately, the wind was howling, and the storm worsened. Determined not to do all the work, Sam taught his grandson to set the jack. Blowing on their hands to keep warm, they loosened the lug nuts, removed the tire, and put on the spare.

Kevin said, "Grandpa, hand me the lug nuts."

Sam patted his jacket pockets, but they weren't there. Despite pawing through the newly fallen snow, their search was fruitless. The missing lug nuts were nowhere to be found. Nearly frost-bitten, they piled into Grandpa's car and drove to the nearest auto parts store. The warm air from the car's heater was a welcomed relief.

Arriving with the new lug nuts and a few extras in case they dropped one in the snow, they attempted to secure the tire on the SUV. Sam sighed heavily, realizing they had inadvertently purchased the wrong size lug nuts.

Sam mumbled in frustration, "Yep, Murphy's Law, anything that can go wrong will go wrong!"

Back at the auto parts store, they purchased another set of new lug nuts; this time, they were the correct size. The tire was successfully mounted, and his grandson was on his way.

When Sam arrived home, his wife, Ruth, wondered where he had been all morning. He'd just left a note that he was going out. As the story unfolded, his wife said, "Why didn't you call the auto club?"

"Oh, I was in a hurry to help him, and honestly, it never even occurred to me," Sam mumbled.

Sam told me he was chilled to the bone, and his wife fed him some warm soup. Then, she offered to cancel his dental appointment. But it looked like the snow was letting up, so Sam insisted he wanted to keep it.

Laughing, Sam said, "I hoped a shower would warm me. As I removed my pants, I heard loud metallic clinks as something spilled onto the hardwood floor. The elusive lug nuts skittered and rolled under the furniture. I tried closing the bedroom door, but Ruth was standing right there shaking her head."

I chuckled as Sam told me Ruth couldn't contain her belly laugh. She said, "Oh, Sam, you are going to owe me big-time for keeping this a secret from Kevin."

36

Showtime

As George entered the dental office, I saw him eyeing my car in the parking lot. He mumbled, "Oh, that car looks familiar. Could it be? I sure hope not."

George grew pale when he saw me looking out my window, checking out his work truck in the office parking lot. Its purple doors emblazoned with the eye-catching company logo make it hard to miss. His van confirmed that George was among the men watching me at Home Depot.

I seated him, and we began chatting. "What have you been up to, George? Buy anything new lately?"

He gulped and looked at me, doing a double take. Then, at a loss for an answer, he stammered, "Um, not really. How about you?"

"Oh, only a six-foot ladder," I commented.

George groaned.

Earlier that week, I had multiple errands to run. Trying to consolidate trips, I loaded my car with items for donation. Then, as I was driving past a Home Depot, I remembered, "Oh, I have to buy that ladder today."

Completely forgetting about my trunk being full, I pulled in and entered the store. After lugging my newly-purchased ladder through the parking lot, I opened the trunk of my small sedan. My eyes widened, and I ran my fingers through my hair while saying a few words under my breath. "Oh my, how could I forget this was supposed to be my last stop? Boy, I'm going to have to be a magician to cram everything in there."

A few rows over, I noticed two men exiting a truck. After seeing my dilemma, I overheard one man say, "Oh, this should be good! She'll never fit that ladder in there. It would be a miracle!"

I guess chivalry is dead because they leaned against the truck with their arms crossed, joking, and waited to watch the show. They were pointing at me to get the attention of other vehicles, and soon others joined the spectators. *Oh, I knew I could prove those doubting construction workers wrong!*

These nonbelievers didn't know they were dealing with a master packer. I moved my daughter to college with this car, and it was amazing what I could squeeze inside. Out of the corner of my eye, I noticed a few other men watching and waiting, including my patient, George, who was now sitting in my dental chair waiting to get his teeth cleaned.

Well, they were in for a treat. I was going to give them a show they wouldn't believe. The ladder now rested against the driver's door. I unpacked the trunk to reposition all the boxes on the left side of the vehicle. Little did my onlookers know that, unlike the standard equipped rear seat with a fixed back, my car had a feature new to vehicles in 1990. I could fold down this seat to accommodate longer cargo. This flexibility allowed me to pack my economy-sized vehicle as tightly as a car full of circus clowns.

I proceeded to fold down the split seat on the right side. Next was my classic trick. I fully reclined the front passenger seat, slid the ladder through, rested the top edge on the dashboard, and easily closed the trunk. Since I was aware I had an audience, I giggled and took a bow to all those men gawking at me.

It was funny to see three trucks of construction workers sitting with their mouths gaping open, shaking their heads. Soon, a man from one of the vehicles approached me and said: "Lady, that was some magic act. I want a car like that!"

My patient, George, apologized for not coming to assist with the ladder. He said, "I was busy joking with the guys. If I knew it was you, I would have helped." However, he did say that I was the talk of Home Depot that week.

I just said. "Open wide, George; I'll try not to hurt you."

37

Critter Hill

When I put my stethoscope around my neck, preparing to take her blood pressure, Janice laughed uncontrollably. "Something must be hilarious to have you laughing so hard," I chuckled.

She replied, "Oh, it is; I'm sorry. Remember the house I told you we were building?"

I remarked, "I was hoping you'd bring pictures. I can't wait to see it."

Janice told me the builder fell way behind schedule, and their apartment lease was up. Since only some outside work remained, the builder agreed to let the newlyweds move in. The young couple was overjoyed.

"Lesson learned," she commented. "When I saw your stethoscope, I couldn't control myself. I have to tell you what happened in our new house." She explained that the porch ceiling needed completion. No one realized that without the bead board in place, an opening from the outside allowed access to a space between the dining room ceiling and the floor joist of the bedroom above. The builder never considered the consequences when he agreed to let them occupy the home early.

"We love sitting on the porch. After a while, a raccoon started hanging around. We're city people, so what did we know about wild animal behavior?" Janice said, laughing.

She continued. "At first, we thought it was cute, but then we noticed she seemed to be getting plumper and plumper. Eventually, one night while we were observing the obviously pregnant animal, she brazenly scooted past our feet and shimmied up the porch post."

On subsequent nights, they saw the same thing happening but never gave it a second thought. "We didn't know there was a space that huge raccoon could squeeze into. Then, after not seeing the mom for a week, we spotted a noticeably thinner animal coming down the post."

"Soon, we heard strange scraping sounds while eating in the dining room. We were at a loss for an explanation until a friend pointed out that the raccoon probably had her babies somewhere in our house." Janice told her that was absurd.

Janice wondered where the raccoon went when it climbed up that post. Upon inspection, they noticed a small gap near the corner of the house. It had to be impossible for an animal that size to squeeze through it, but sounds were getting louder each day.

She borrowed a stethoscope from work, climbed a ladder, and started listening to the ceiling in her dining room. Sure enough, she heard faint crying noises. Janice called the builder, and he called animal control. She wondered, "How are we going to get them out?"

The next day a strange-looking van with pictures of animals on the doors pulled into the driveway. It looked like an advertisement for a traveling zoo. Even stranger looking was the character emerging from the van dressed in a buckskin vest partially covered with fringe and a coonskin cap complete with tail. "I'm the critter removal specialist," He proudly announced. "How can I help you?"

Andrew and Janice looked at each other, trying to hide their smirks. They told him their suspicions, and after examining the gap, the man told them the raccoon had probably found the perfect nesting place.

The garage and the dining room had a common wall, and the frontiersman cut an access hole in the garage's ceiling. Then, he climbed up a ladder in the garage and stuck his head in the opening to look around.

Janice screamed, "Are you crazy putting your unprotected head in a space where a mother is defending her babies?"

The critter guy just laughed. He shined a flashlight and could see the movement, but luckily, the mother wasn't there. He remarked, "Raccoons usually only have one or two babies, but this mama had a bunch."

"Wonderful," Janice groaned.

Janice, Andrew, and the exterminator all worked together to get the exact location of the babies before the mother returned. Janice was back on the ladder with her stethoscope. Andrew gave location coordinates by calling out which floor joist bays the sound was loudest, and the critter man used his tool with a loop on the end to snag the babies.

It was quite a production. After successfully removing six tiny raccoons and a seventh that didn't survive, the man in the coon cap asked if he could strike a bargain. He explained, "My wife's favorite animal is the raccoon, and I won't charge you if I can keep this liter." Andrew shrieked, "Take them, please, take them as far away from here as possible." All the newlyweds wanted was a rodent-free home.

The raccoon man's wife was in the truck crying because she feared they would hurt her little bundles of fur. "What a strange pair," Janice thought. "He's dressed all in animal fur, and she wants to save every animal possible."

The exterminator promised to take the babies to a place called Critter Hill, far from where they were born. The whole thing sounded bizarre to Andrew and Janice, but they agreed as long he promised the raccoons were never returning.

Coon man explained, "I have to set a cage to trap the mother. I'll put it into the ceiling opening and come back for her."

Janice asked, "How will we know the mom is trapped?"

He replied, "Believe me, you won't need that stethoscope, you'll know. The cage will rattle, with such a racket crying for her babies that you won't be able to stand it."

The critter specialist promised to nurse the babies until he could reunite the family. In the following weeks, the builder closed up the openings, and he learned a valuable lesson: not to let owners move in before the house was complete.

Janice finished her unusual story, and I finally got to use my stethoscope and blood pressure cuff. To this day, I smile every time I look at it and remember the crazy raccoon story.

38

Reality TV

Sarah, my dental patient, is the camp director for children with special needs. Six months ago, she was bubbling with the news that an accessible tree house at the Sunshine Camp was in the planning stages, and the project would be on an episode of HGTV.

Today when she arrived, she had her dad with her. He took the time slot after her appointment, so they both came into the treatment room. I couldn't wait to ask, "Well, how did the filming go?"

She replied, "It's so completely different, more than you imagine. Beefur, how's that for a name? He's the lead carpenter and has a quick wit. He's always cracking jokes. I guess you need that type of personality to pull off a reality show. The entire experience was eye-opening."

"What do you mean?"

She giggled. "The real-time shots are retaken over and over until the so-called spontaneous reaction you see on the show is achieved. Nothing is real on reality TV."

Sarah laughed again and explained, "Adlibbing isn't easy. I wish I had a script. My role would have been a lot easier. My dad got to work on the tree house project with me, but it wasn't his first experience with reality TV."

"Well, you have my undivided attention."

I started cleaning Sarah's teeth, and her dad, Butch, took over the conversation. "I think my buddies and I were the first reality fakes."

"I hope you're going to explain," I chuckled.

"Well, I was stationed in Alaska in 1968. It was a hunter's paradise! Each time I had a few days off, my buddies and I headed up the Richardson Highway in search of moose and caribou.

Sarah tried to talk. "Grling..ghrkgh."

I removed my hands from her mouth, and she said, "Dad, what does that have to do with reality TV?"

I was intrigued, too. My dental patients always have the best stories!

"I'm getting to that," her dad explained. "We were hunting on the frozen tundra and were ecstatic to have bagged four caribou with impressive antlers. We field-dressed them but left the skinning till we were someplace warmer. We didn't want to encounter a grizzly bear looking for a meal."

I listened as he conveyed the rest of the tale.

"It was twenty below zero with limited daylight. We were heading back to camp when a caravan of Willys jeeps identical to ours approached. There was a local broadcast network logo on the doors. A cameraman flagged us down."

Sarah gurgled.

Butch continued, "In Alaska, not stopping to help a motorist in the winter is illegal since it's not only sub-zero but pitch black outside for months."

Participating in the three-way conversation made it difficult to get my work done.

Butch said, "The cameraman's eyes about bugged out as he yelled, 'Looks like you guys had a great hunt! We're trying to shoot a hunting documentary. We're frozen and haven't seen a living animal. Any chance you soldiers would like to help us out?'"

It was Butch's turn in the chair, but Sarah remembered the rest of the story.

"Dad struck a deal. What transpired next was surreal:

1. The TV crew packed the carcasses of the dead caribou with snow to plump them up and cleaned any sign of blood off the fur.
2. They fabricated makeshift saw horses from tree branches.
3. Four dead caribou were propped up to look as realistic as possible."

"That's incredible!" I commented as Butch made me take my hands out of his mouth.

Butch wanted to tell the rest of the story. "The film crew captured the hunters skillfully shooting the already dead caribou. Rigging ropes were attached to the branches, so the crew could make caribou fall when shot. Then with creative editing and telephoto lenses, the filmmakers portrayed a realistic-looking hunt."

Sarah laughed, "Voila, the hunting expedition bagged their limit of trophy caribou!"

Butch added between rinses, "The show aired and became an overnight success. Understandably, only a few of us were privy to the real story. We got a great lump of money, but secrecy was part of the deal."

I was amused. "Forty-six years later, who's going to know?"

Sarah retorted, "I guess this proves reality TV is as far from reality as you can get."

39

Swinging Pineapple

I was surprised to see Rose's name on my schedule. Rose relocated to Florida last year, but her dream of a perfect retirement vanished when she lost her husband six months after they moved. When she came in, I greeted her with a hug.

"Rose, it's so good to see you. Are you visiting your daughter?"

"No, I'm back for good!" she said empathically. "I'll NEVER return to that crazy place!"

"Rose, what happened? You and Simon were so excited. It must be awful without him, but I thought you still loved it."

In a quivering voice, Rose said, "Oh, I did, but let me tell you why I'm back."

From previous conversations, I knew Rose's husband, Simon, was anxious to make Florida their new home. For three years, they researched and visited various areas of the state. Ultimately, the appeal of this self-contained community in Central Florida, featuring excellent shopping, premier golf courses, and five-star restaurants, won their hearts.

Balmy weather, maintenance-free condos, and no more snow to shovel outweighed the fifty-page homeowner's rules manual that accompanied the sales agreement. There were stringent regulations about everything imaginable. Rose's main objection was the endless set of rules concerning grandchildren. Rose and Simon had some serious discussions, but the enticement of a community clubhouse with every imaginable activity offset the rules.

Rose reminisced, "Simon enjoyed one last woodworking project before he packed up his tools for the move. After he checked the handbook to be sure signs were permitted, he hand-carved the time-honored symbol of southern hospitality for the front entry. It's gorgeous and was his best work."

Teary-eyed Rose said, "I decided I had to continue this next chapter of my life, but I never dreamed it would be without Simon. We hadn't even completely unpacked."

Rose's daughter, Tracey, came to visit and helped her mom sort through the rest of the neglected boxes. Tracey came across the beautiful wooden plaque her father had made. Rose had never seen it completed and was emotionally overcome by the inscription on the back. It read; *My dear Rose, wishing us health and happiness in our new home.*

Tracey and her mom both had a good cry. Then, grabbing the toolbox, and the step stool, Tracey hammered a nail with the sun shining on her back and hung the pineapple sign. Tracey commented, "Mom, this will make you feel like Dad is always with you."

Rose turned to me, and to my surprise, she said, "The crowning blow was when I displayed my welcome sign."

I looked at her with a question on my lips, but she continued.

"When I returned from driving Tracey to the airport, a man sat on my stoop, waiting for me. He insisted that he wanted to come inside for coffee. I managed to side-step around him and send him on his way."

Rose said, "I thought that was peculiar, but this was just the beginning, and things got stranger. Almost every day, another man dressed in similar attire---plaid shorts, striped shirt, sandals, and black socks, pulled up his golf cart and asked to come into my house. I was getting tired of these intrusions."

Rose continued, "I peeked through the blinds to see another suitor had arrived, so I flung open the door. The man was about to speak, but I blurted out, "I just buried my husband. I'm not looking for a man. Please, I want to be left alone."

Perplexed, he replied, "You're not? Well, your sign says differently."

She asked, "What do you mean? What sign?" Now it was Rose's turn to be puzzled.

He pointed to the pineapple plaque proudly hanging above her front entrance.

"The pineapple?"

He was still pointing. "No, the swingers sign?"

What? What are you talking about?" Rose asked, utterly baffled.

"The pineapple signifies a swinger lives here," he said, as Rose noticed a pineapple patch emblem on his shirt.

"A swinger?" Rose gasped. "Oh my goodness! Where I moved from, a pineapple simply means WELCOME."

Rose forcefully slammed the door. She immediately located the step stool. After making sure the latest gigolo was gone, Rose removed the sign. "Simon would think that was a hoot!" she laughed with sadness in her eyes.

Rose and I were now laughing. "I called the realtor and began packing that very day, so here I am, back in frigid Rochester."

40

The Michelin Man

It was Christmas time, and a man dressed as Santa was a common sight. One Jolly Old St. Nick entered our office, ho-ho-ho-ing. He addressed us by name as if he knew us forever. His timing was perfect, not interrupting our busy patient schedule.

The five of us all looked at each other. With the kindhearted personal greetings Santa gave each of us, we all thought the others knew our man in the red suit. He said he was collecting for a well-known charity that provides much-needed services, helping veterans, especially during the holidays.

We all dug in our purses, not wanting to appear rude, giving him generous donations. We didn't have any inkling that something was amiss. But after he left, I had a nagging uncomfortable feeling. I asked, "Which of our patients was perky St. Nick? I'm so embarrassed that I didn't recognize Santa."

We all looked at each other again, not smiling this time. Feeling foolish, we hoped we were wrong, but "scam" was written all over it. A visit from the police, who had received complaints from other building tenants, confirmed we were correct in our assumption.

I spoke, "Unfortunately, we waited until he left to question his identity."

The policeman said, "I give Santa credit; he spoke to you like old friends after reading your name tags. There is no telling how much money he pocketed."

A few weeks later, we learned that all the offices visited by Santa had reported a burglary over the Christmas holidays.

Dr. Richards, our boss, is a black belt in karate. Concerned for our safety, he asked his instructor, Carolyn, if she would give his staff private self-defense lessons. Bursting with energy, we donned our yoga pants. Five awkward students showed up for the six weeks of private classes. The Martial Arts training taught us to be constantly aware of our surroundings.

Carolyn explained, "Contrary to popular belief, thrusting a knee to the groin is not the best defense since it will make the perpetrator lunge toward you. Instead, the preferred moves are to gouge the eyes or kick with the ball of the foot to the solar plexus. These movements are ideal; they throw off the assailant's center of gravity."

"I'm so proud of all of us," I told Dr. Richards. "My newly attained self-defense skills really boosted my self-confidence."

On the last day of class, each of us had to fend off an attacker. Camera in hand, Dr. Richards took a seat in the bleachers. He said, "I can't wait to see you in action."

Sensei Carolyn reminded us, "You need to practice your moves, but remember to demonstrate, not actually perform the techniques."

A colossal man, the size of a sumo wrestler, faced the class. He wore a heavily padded shiny silver suit and headgear similar to a hockey player's helmet.

"Doesn't he remind you of the Michelin Man?" I commented as we all stared at the strange sight.

I waited with my back turned, aware that at any minute, the trainer would attack me. I wondered how I would react if I didn't know an assault was coming. I understood a direct attack was imminent, yet he still took me by complete surprise.

Somehow, my auto-pilot kicked in. I performed my favorite move, the hip twist. A fake kick to the quadriceps followed by a pretend eye gouge followed to finish him off. Theoretically, now I could flee. "That was much harder than I thought," I told my friend Regina.

I turned to my co-workers, "I was totally unprepared for being rammed with such brute force. It sure was a rude awakening."

The testing continued. We all did remarkably well for amateurs. Regina was the last to demonstrate her skills. She had watched intently as we all adequately defended ourselves. Noticing that none of us used the foot-stomping move, Regina prepared to prove she was also competent. Michelin-man drew near and accosted her. Regina swiveled her hips, lifted her foot, and stomped with all her might. Oops…she forgot this was a drill.

Across the studio, we heard a bone-chilling snap. Shrieking cries of agony came from the shiny silver man. Quite a scene ensued as he grimaced in pain. Regina shot a horrified glance at us as she contritely approached the injured fellow.

Hobbling and limping, the man quickly backed away from Regina as she tried to extend an apology. "I'm so sorry! I forgot!"

The Michelin Man scowled at Dr. Richards, whose eyes danced with amusement because he knew he had captured Regina's incident on film. A large framed photo is on the wall in our dental office, and our boss, a flawless storyteller, narrated the story to any patient who listened.

41

Thumbs Up

The dental office where I worked was on the same country road as my house. After work, I left the office parking lot and noticed a pickup truck in the distance. I knew that I had plenty of space to pull out. However, the driver must have thought otherwise because he blasted the horn, and the truck began gaining speed, barreling forward. Looking in the rearview mirror, I began to smile, thinking this was my son-in-law's truck, and he was fooling around.

It soon became evident this wasn't my son-in-law but some lunatic trying to run me off the road. He was obviously impatient with my 4-cylinder car's speed because the truck came very close to my bumper, and now he was trying to ram me. If you are wondering why I didn't call for help, this incident happened in pre-cell phone times.

I gunned the accelerator, causing the car to speed up considerably, but it wasn't satisfactory to the big black truck. The truck horn began blaring. As much as I yearned for the safety of my home, I didn't want to pull into my driveway, letting him know where I lived. Being a safe yet defensive driver is challenging to implement when road rage is involved, so I took my first evasive action to escape his fury by turning practically on two wheels at the first crossroad past my house.

His car was in hot pursuit; the chase went on, and I was at his mercy.

Somehow I managed to lose him, but as I went over the next hill, I realized he had circled back and was waiting for me.

He continued to chase me. I was petrified and began praying out loud. When he passed me, I thought he must have gotten tired of the game, but my relief was short-lived when I realized he was in front of me now. He was driving fast and then slamming on the brakes, trying to cause a rear-end collision making me at fault.

My mind was wielding irrational thoughts. In desperation, I raised my hand, shaking my fist like a windshield wiper, trying to execute an obscene hand gesture. It was so out of character for me that I honestly didn't know which finger to put in the air. Thinking I had to do something, I shook my fist wildly.

I was acting like a crazy person, and then I realized I had done the exact opposite of what I intended. With my shaking hand, I noticed that I just gave him "the thumb" in a thumbs-up sign. So much for *flipping the bird!*

My survival instincts were on full alert. The driver's mistake of passing me allowed me to turn at a more reasonable speed on the next road and escape. Unless he made a U-turn, his next intersecting road was a few miles away. Frazzled, I drove around for a long time before heading home and pulling my car into the garage.

From that day forward, my family always took the opportunity when they felt like stooping to "flick someone off" to say, "Just give 'em the thumb," and we all understood.

42

The Fickle Finger of Fate

Early Sunday morning, I arrived at church, and my co-worker Regina started telling me about her drive home the day before.

"Was Saturday the day for crazies?" she asked. She told me she was heading home from her daughter's house on the interstate when a black BMW with heavily tinted windows started weaving in and out of the busy weekend traffic and seemed to have her as a target.

"I couldn't get away from this reckless driver. The car stayed neck and neck with me for miles as it cut in and out of the stream of traffic."

"Regina, a driver like that makes me so nervous," I commented.

Regina sighed, "This erratic driving continued, and I was thrilled to see my exit ramp ahead. The BMW passed in the far left lane and looked like he would continue straight. Unfortunately, the car swerved over three lanes in front of me to get off the same exit, just about putting me in the ditch. We stopped at the adjacent toll booths, and the BMW's window rolled down. I was astonished that the driver was female, and she looked over at me, smirking."

"Normally, using obscene hand gestures would never even enter my mind, but this terrifying incident really made me lose my composure. I found myself in a situation where instinct took over. I was like a mama bear protecting her cub since my granddaughter was in my car. It just happened! I looked the nasty driver directly in the eyes, and with a determined controlled gesture, I raised my middle finger and 'flipped her the bird.'"

My mouth dropped open since this was so uncharacteristic of meek, soft-spoken Regina. But instead, I laughed and thought *she could have given her the thumb.*

Chuckling, Regina added, "At that same moment, a sense of dreaded recognition came over me as I realized this driver was a church member. I exited the toll road, angry but embarrassed. I let the BMW disappear into the sea of cars. Silently I prayed that my granddaughter wasn't paying attention."

Regina told me she moaned as she glanced into the backseat. "Thank heavens, my sweet granddaughter was asleep. I tried to rationalize that the probability of a close encounter with the same 'mad woman' was slim."

Regrettably, the very next day, at Mass, this hypothesis proved to be inaccurate. It was Regina's Sunday to serve as Eucharistic minister, and when she took her place at the altar, I saw Regina's worried expression as she scanned the worshippers. I wondered if the increasing intensity of the thunderstorm outside worried her.

Later I learned that the BMW lady was standing in her line. "What am I going to do?" I heard her mumble. Reverently, the wild driver approached the altar. To avoid recognition, Regina tried not to make eye contact.

At the precise moment, Regina placed the host in the crazy lady's hands, a powerful bolt of lightning struck the church, hitting the steeple right above the altar. Everyone in line jumped as the rain began to soak the congregation.

The severe storm that developed during the service created quite a commotion. Regina felt this was a sign of punishment for her transgression. The terrified crowd darted from the church. Utter pandemonium ensued, and she lost sight of the lady.

We replayed these incidents at work on Monday, recalling all the details for Dr. Richards. Regina told the boss, "I have no idea if the woman realized I was the one that gave her *the finger*, but I felt as if the lightning was going to strike me. I know it's a sign from God that I need to repent."

Later that year, an interesting twist developed. Regina injured her right hand, and the treatment was to splint her middle finger in the "obscene gesture" position. Ironically, it remained that way for three months. Regina never knew if this was God's way of punishing her or just the *fickle finger of fate.*

43

Don't Fool with the Master

I worked for Dr. Richards for twenty-five years, and in that time, he never missed an opportunity to execute one of his outrageous practical jokes. He could turn a seemingly innocent occurrence into a mischievous event. His patients came to hear his stories as much as for his excellent dentistry.

Everyone in Rochester, New York, received a notice from the phone company announcing we had to change our area code. We all dreaded this mandate: however, the staff saw this as our opportunity, and for once, we decided to pull a practical joke on Dr. Richards.

Taking the letter from the phone company and performing some creative alterations, we printed a document that appeared to be very official and authentic. We knew Dr. Richards would open the mail and be the first to see this notice. Our prank correspondence explained that our new phone number would contain twenty-one digits. It went something like 585-334-445-236-478-209-777.

He was infuriated and dialed the phone company himself, demanding an explanation. As Dr. Richards ranted to the customer service representative, in her "customer is always right voice," she tried to be polite to this lunatic. Even after speaking to a supervisor, he still couldn't find anyone to sympathize or understand his complaint. He was fuming, and we were fearful he would have a stroke, so we had to come clean. Finally, Dr. Richards had to admit we beat him in his own game. It left us with great satisfaction... until the next day.

He planned his retaliation because he couldn't let our prank pass without revenge.

Our receptionist ordered a sandwich deli tray for our office meeting. Dr. Richards insisted on picking it up on his way to work, a task he usually delegated to someone else. I should have been suspicious from the beginning since the restaurant was out of his way, and I passed right by it on my way to work.

We all went to the break room, loaded our plates, and settled in for another boring office meeting. The plan almost backfired as Dr. Richards watched everyone choose the rolls with cheddar slices, that is, until I took a Ham and Swiss sandwich. Now, he was grinning.

I tried to be polite but couldn't bite into the cheese. I tugged and pulled to no avail. Being a hygienist, I knew each tooth had a different function, so I moved my sandwich from my front teeth to the canines meant for tearing. I thought maybe this crusty Ciabatta roll was the culprit, but I noticed no one else was having trouble.

My co-workers were stared at me, trying to figure out what I was doing. By this time, Dr. Richards could not contain himself. He loved a good laugh, and he was unquestionably having one. Soon the laughter became contagious because I looked so ridiculous attacking this sandwich, yet no one understood the scope of my problem.

Unbeknownst to the staff, Dr. Richards had visited a novelty store and purchased rubbery, plastic Swiss cheese slices. They looked very realistic. He had put them in a package of aged Swiss cheese for the night, so they looked real and smelled edible.

Through his laughter, the boss willingly confessed when my confusion was evident. He was delighted that he had two more stories to entertain his patients.

I looked at Dr. Richards and threw my hands up in the air. "You win! I guess we'll never outdo the Master!"

PART THREE

Rochester, New York

1991-2005

(Years overlap-working in two offices)

44

Opportunity Comes Knocking

Our dinner was on the table, but a loud shouting and persistent pounding on the door disturbed our evening. "Please, I need help," a young woman cried out.

It was a snowy, blustery night, and I was glad my husband and I were safe at home. The howling winds, whipping across our seven-hundred-foot-long driveway, were especially vicious. The weatherman had predicted the storm but forecasted it to begin after midnight. Instead, blizzard conditions had started early in the day, catching people off guard.

We lived on a well-traveled country road where the houses were sparse. The year was 1991, so cell phones had yet to debut. Since the nearest gas station was about five miles away, we often had people stop to ask for help.

Kelly showed up on my doorstep, looking nearly frozen. There was no hesitation in letting the girl in the house. With her teeth chattering, she managed to say, "Thank you so much! My car slid off the road into a ditch. As I trudged through the snow, I spotted a car pulling in this driveway."

"Are you okay? Do I need to call 911?"

"No, I'm not hurt. My dad drives a tow truck. Can I call my mom?" Kelly made a phone call. "Mom is frantic, praying to hear from me. She is relieved I'm safe."

I had barely made it home from work myself and was still in my scrubs. However, I couldn't help but notice my visitor also wore scrubs. So I asked, "Do you work around here?"

Kelly said, "I'm a dental assistant working for Dr. Smiley. She just opened a dental practice down the road." Still shivering, Kelly continued, "I was trying to walk back to the office when I realized it's too far, and I don't have a key. I'm sure everyone has already left for the day. I didn't know what I was going to do."

With the weather deteriorating, it took quite a while for help to arrive. I gave Kelly a blanket and some hot tea while we waited. We chatted as Kelly thawed.

I chuckled, "Dr. Smiley, what an appropriate name for a dentist."

I explained, "Actually, I am a Dental Hygienist. I heard a dentist recently opened her practice near here. Would you be so kind as to give my name and number to your boss?" Kelly was quick to agree.

I added, "I work part-time in Rochester, but I'd love to add a few more days. Your boss is probably not in the market to hire a hygienist yet, but I'd appreciate the opportunity to interview for the position when she's ready."

Kelly's mom accompanied her dad in the tow truck. Her mother was gushing with relief when she saw her daughter. As her mom embraced her daughter, she said, "Kelly is only eighteen, and this is her first job. I was so worried."

Having two teenage daughters, I could appreciate her mother's concern.

One day, I received a phone call from Kelly. She said, "I told Dr. Smiley how nice you are. She is very interested in speaking with you."

A week later, I went on an interview and was hired on the spot. My new employers said, "It will be an asset to have someone with strong connections to the local community working here."

Sometimes you don't have to travel far for an employment opportunity; sometimes, it just comes knocking on your door.

45

Building a Friendship

It was moving day. We were relocating from Buffalo to Rochester, New York, only a ninety-mile distance, but I worried about coping with young children with no family nearby. I was used to a large circle of friends and family as a support system.

While we emptied the moving van, a neighbor approached and offered to have our children play together so we could unpack. We had temporarily rented a townhouse, and I could see the girls playing, so I took her up on her generous offer.

We soon found we had similar interests. Our new friends had also moved into the townhouses while building. We learned that both our husbands are skilled carpenters and decided to complete all the construction phases by doing the work on our permanent homes themselves.

Knowing that we were not the only ones attempting such a monumental undertaking was comforting. It took about eighteen months to finalize the carpentry, plumbing, electrical, and drywall. So our bond grew as we put in hours of heavy labor each night and every weekend.

Sometimes, we were so overwhelmed that we just hung out together to regroup. Other times, we took turns helping each other through critical building stages. Finally, we each got our certificates of occupancy and were overjoyed to move into our homes.

One day, after her dental appointment, Anna told me her dentist was looking to hire a hygienist. I commented that this was probably the same office where the dental assistant stranded in the storm worked. The other exciting detail was that this dentist had a new office only five miles down the road, and I would be the first hygienist if hired. This opportunity would ease the strain that building put on our budget, and I was looking forward to meeting people in our new community.

"Is your dentist's name Dr. Smiley?"

Anna nodded.

The morning of the interview, I called Anna, and she sounded horrible. She had a high fever and body aches and told me she had been sick for days. I had the ingredients for the sure-cure of chicken soup and made a pot.

I went to the interview and was elated that I got the job. It was perfect, just a few days a week, and I could have the school bus drop the girls off at Anna's until I got out of work two hours later.

I drove over to Anna's with my soup and good news. We had given each other keys, and I let myself in when she didn't answer my knock. I put the soup on the counter and was ready to call out when I saw the strangest sight. I almost started laughing but then realized the gravity of the situation.

As I stood in my friend's kitchen, through the window, I saw her outside at the top of a twelve-foot ladder in a red, one-piece pajama complete with attached booties. Anna was attempting to put her leg up and hoist herself into a partially opened window on the second story of her house. It seemed ludicrous because the window was not a double-hung but a narrow window that cranked out. I had no idea how Anna would ever fit through that window opening or how she managed to maneuver that heavy ladder herself. Besides, the deck was covered in ice and snow, and an unstable ladder was an accident waiting to happen.

I didn't want to startle her since the ladder was directly in front of her kitchen window. So I slowly opened the sliding glass door on her deck. Anna turned with relief across her face and started crying.

Anna told me that her fever spiked, and she went out to the car to get the aspirin she had purchased a few days ago when she locked herself out of the house. We each had built in the country on ten-acre lots, so no neighbors were nearby to help. It was frigid out, and it would be hours before anyone would be home.

I helped her down and into the house, heated the soup, and put her to bed. Then, I waited for the school bus so her children would come to my house and she could rest.

That fateful day was forty years ago, but it seems like yesterday. We reminisce that as we built our homes with hammers and saws, we also created the foundation of a strong friendship that has withstood the test of time.

46

Hole-y Drywall

It was still dark as I arrived at work. I thought *it was a full moon, and today is Friday the 13th*. What a combination! It was a predictable fact; we always had the weirdest things happen with our patients when the moon was full. "I'm sure this will be an interesting day," I said aloud.

I noticed huge boxes of paper towels from yesterday's delivery were still cluttering the hallway. Before I could say a word, Nancy, our newly hired dental assistant, attempted to carry one of the bulky boxes down the basement stairs. Finding the load too cumbersome, she shoved the box, watching it tumble end over end. I could hear the thumping as it plummeted, but then I heard a loud crash, and Nancy gasped. The box punched a massive hole in the newly installed paneling. Panicking, Nancy rushed down to assess the damage.

I yelled down the stairs, "Are you okay?"

"Not really!" she cried.

Nancy flew up the stairs, causing her toe to catch on the top step. She landed flat on her face in the narrow hallway slamming her head through the drywall. She was pale as a ghost and disoriented. I called 911. While paramedics assessed her for injuries, she was inconsolable. Nancy sobbed, saying, "I'm going to get fired. I broke the wall. I broke two walls."

Nancy was shaken but not severely injured, so she stayed and worked. We couldn't wait for Friday the 13th to be over, and it was only 8:00 a.m.

Our first patient Sally was a heavyset, elderly woman and the most superstitious person I had ever met. She arrived at her appointment visibly upset.

She moaned, "While trying to dodge a black cat from running in front of me, I accidentally walked under a ladder."

"Sally, that sounds like your worst nightmare! I can't believe you would make an appointment on Friday the 13th!"

She shrugged her shoulders. It was time for me to clean her teeth. Sally had mobility issues, so shifting her onto the seat was especially difficult because this dental chair's design was less than ideal. Worse yet, the new cleaning crew had waxed the chair, unbeknownst to me.

Sally backed up to the chair, trying to navigate the protruding arm that did not fold down for easy transfer. She attempted to position her oversized derriere correctly on the dental chair but found it challenging. Then, as Sally plopped her behind where the chair was already beginning to slope, her polyester skirt and the slippery chair proved to be a bad combination. Before Sally could swing her legs around, she started to slide down the chair, gaining momentum with every inch.

Both of us were now screaming while I watched in horror. Time seemed to stand still. With a four-pronged cane still in her hand, Sally thrust it forward to brace against the wall. Instead of stopping herself, she only made matters worse. Her body weight jammed the cane against her ribs, puncturing the drywall. It protruded from the wall while the patient was trapped in a precarious position on the floor, wedged between the chair and the counter. She was stuck and groaning. Paramedics came again.

My boss said, "Look at the colossal size of that hole."

I said, "Maybe there is something to this superstition. I hope Sally didn't crack a rib."

Even though she was injured and distraught, the superstitious Sally insisted that the paramedics remove her from the office by the same door she used to enter. The EMTs looked puzzled.

I explained, "The old wives tale states you must always enter and leave by the same door, or bad luck will follow." It was not worth upsetting her anymore, so instead of exiting through the back door, they pushed Sally, on a gurney, through a waiting room full of patients.

Dr. Smiley groaned, "How much more bad luck could any of us have today?"

I answered, "If I recall superstitions, bad luck comes in threes. Let's all hope the three holes in the wall count, so we don't have to call the paramedics for the third time because we still have a long day ahead of us."

We worked the rest of the day with our fingers crossed, which is particularly difficult when you are working in someone's mouth.

47

White Coat Syndrome

Millions of people experience physical symptoms such as a spike in blood pressure or profuse sweating when they enter any medical facility. Doctors referred to this as *White Coat Syndrome.* Dr. Smiley had one particular patient that stands out in my mind.

Lisa was the most extreme example of this phenomenon I have ever encountered. It was difficult for her to even pull into the parking lot of any medical office complex, and a dental office sent her anxiety levels off the charts.

Maintaining good oral health was critical after Lisa was diagnosed with heart disease. Untreated gum disease can affect the entire body, and it was crucial for Lisa to seek dental treatment. Her health depended on dealing with her trepidation.

Lisa didn't hesitate to call Dr. Smiley for help. Lisa pleaded, "Please, I need to get my teeth fixed. This fear that grips me is so real. How am I going to do this?"

Knowing that phobic patients commonly need extensive treatment, Dr. Smiley explained, "Lisa, I know it has been years since you've been in the office. I suggest we start with a therapist specializing in the treatment of phobias. I know a great one that is in the next building."

On our recommendation, all-encompassing counseling sessions and behavior management began:

> Step one: was to drive by the office daily for a few weeks.
> Step two: park and remain in her car.
> Step three: required Lisa to enter the reception area and stay awhile.

This conditioning therapy process took months, but the day came for step four. Lisa was to sit in the dental chair. She would come in on our lunch hour, sit in a dental chair and meditate. The first time, Lisa was there only a minute before she bolted, but after multiple visits, she managed to stay the entire hour. Now Lisa was ready to make an appointment for an exam and x-rays.

When Lisa arrived, I reassured her we would go slowly. I wondered if she was ready to have me put my hands in her mouth. I administered the Nitrous Oxide, more commonly known as "laughing gas," but it seemed to have little effect. It's supposed to calm the patient and make them comfortable. When Lisa stuck out her tongue, I held it with gauze as I examined her soft tissue. Then she clamped her mouth shut.

"Lisa, that was a great start. Are you ready to continue?"

She opened her mouth ever so slightly, and I cautiously slid my tiny mirror along her cheek.

Without warning, her teeth chomped down on my mouth mirror. I had to pry her teeth apart because fear paralyzed her. "Stop, please stop. I can't do this yet," the distraught patient screamed, and she jumped out of the chair, ripping the hose for the Nitrous gas. I quickly shut off the tank valve as the entire room filled with laughing gas.

"Lisa, thank heaven I have quick reflexes, or you would have bitten my fingers."

I laughed and hoped that was a natural reaction, not the laughing gas's effect on me. As I opened a window to air out the room, I knew I had to think of another approach.

We set up another appointment. The most we could accomplish was a quick exam, but we took baby steps each visit. Taking Lisa's mind off her fears was challenging, but I had a plan. I told Lisa to bring her iPod and choose relaxing music she liked, but the songs must be ones she would only listen to at her appointments. It would be her therapy music because I didn't want her favorite songs to remind her of the dentist.

The next visit, before she could have a panic attack, I put on the laughing gas mask on Lisa. She was wearing her headphones, already listening to music, just as I had instructed. It was the perfect distraction.

That's good, Lisa. Breathe deep, and let the laughing gas do its job. Keep taking deep breaths in and out."

I liberally swabbed topical anesthetic on her gums to work its magic along with the laughing gas. Lisa was thrilled no needles were involved. Before she could protest, I told her I would use a child-size mouth prop. I explained it was a flexible rubber wedge to keep her mouth open.

She agreed, saying, "I was so worried I would bite you."

I assured Lisa, "I learned fast. It only took getting bitten once to make me conscious of keeping my fingers safe."

Every two weeks, we had Lisa come back for short appointments. She never conceded that she enjoyed these visits, but her anxiety level was lower, and she seemed less stressed.

Lisa never overcame her White Coat Syndrome, and her heart still raced when she walked in the door. I believe it was our compassion and understanding of her feelings that made her one of our most compliant patients. However, she always wore her running shoes, just in case she had to make a quick getaway and escape.

48

Unexpected Lockup

The final phase of our office expansion was done after office hours to avoid inconveniences to the staff or patients. Unfortunately, the construction workers failed to realize this was a dental office with areas requiring a clean, sterile environment.

I arrived at work and checked each room, and it was the first morning I could turn on all the equipment without a single glitch. "Wow, everything seems to be in order," I said aloud. "It looks like it promises to be a good day."

My co-workers and I were thrilled to have an employee restroom. I noticed the lock on the door was in place as I entered the new space. I cringed as the spring-loaded door slammed behind me, and I made a mental note to have the contractors adjust this hinge.

When I was ready to leave the restroom, to my horror, the door knob didn't turn. *No, this can't be happening.* I tried again. Nothing I did would open the door, and I was all alone. I wasn't hysterical because I knew my co-workers would be there soon, but I was panicky because my first patient was due to arrive. I waited but never heard a sound until Stacy, another hygienist, came about fifteen minutes later.

Expecting to see me in my treatment room, she called out, "Terry, where are you?"

"I'm locked in the bathroom!" I shouted. "The door won't open. I've tried everything."

Stacy tried the handle but failed. It wouldn't budge. "This could only happen to you," she said, laughing out loud.

Any humor in this situation had long since passed for me. My voice quivered, "I rummaged through this storage cabinet, looking for something I could use, but my hairbrush was the only 'tool' I could find." So frantically, I continued banging. "I've been pounding, trying to raise the pins in the hinges. I'm not having much luck."

Stacy continued to laugh.

I implored, "Please try to use a credit card or butter knife to spring the lock."

Unlike the magical release of the lock in the movies, nothing happened. I was still trapped. Stacy said, "You remind me of the TV character MacGyver."

"Really?" I said sarcastically. "How do you think MacGyver would get this door open?"

My first patient arrived twenty minutes late and was in the waiting room. "Great," I mumbled. "It's pretty obvious I can't see him."

He peered down the hall, wondering what was causing the racket. Then seeing the situation, he couldn't help but laugh. Offering assistance, my patient suggested, "I have a small Swiss Army Knife. See if this does the trick." He slipped it under the door.

"Thanks," I said. My hairbrush had already proved ineffective, and I was ready to try something else. I hesitated as I looked over the Swiss Army Knife knock-off. It had a screwdriver, but it didn't look too sturdy. *The last thing I want today is to replace his knife.*

Stacy cleaned my patient's teeth while I tried to break out of the bathroom. I struggled using the fragile penknife. It was useless.

When my patient was ready to leave, he said, "Sorry, Terry, I'm going to need my knife back."

I slid his knife under the door. "Thanks; I was hoping this would work."

"Is there anything else I can do?

I sniffled, holding back the tears. "No, I guess we'll have to call someone. Thanks so much."

He apologized, "Sorry, it didn't help. Bye! Thanks for the great story I'll have to tell at the office."

Stacy explained my predicament as the staff clocked in. I heard the unmistakable sounds of amusement grow louder. Dr. Smiley was taking off her coat. "What's all the giggling about?"

Stacy couldn't resist, "We're just making fun of Terry. She's locked in the bathroom pretending she's MacGyver."

After my boss stopped laughing, she grew increasingly aggravated at the construction worker's apparent slip-up. Clutching the office phone, she dialed the project manager. She blasted him, "Who would install a lock without checking it was functional?"

After a very long ninety minutes, two crew members showed up. The foreman said, "I don't know how we are going to get her out of there since the hinges are on the inside." Those weren't words I wanted to hear. I yelled through the door. "H-e-l-l-o---I can hear you!"

It was now over three hours since I had become imprisoned. Dumb and Dumber were trying to figure out how to set me free. Their strategy was to demolish the new door. I suggested taking a hammer to the handle instead. The lock came apart as I knew it would, and I was sprung. Freedom came just in the nick of time because I was at the end of my rope.

The dental supply salesman stopped by that day while I was in lockup. Grabbing his order forms, he was in a rush to leave. He called his dispatcher with the story, and it spread like wildfire. The gossip hotline buzzed as every dentist in a two-hundred-mile radius heard about my dilemma. No matter where I went in the dental community, someone would stop me and say, "Oh, so you're the one."

Life was finally getting back to normal. Six months passed when the office staff traveled to a dental convention across the country. We were all excited to be in Las Vegas. At our first workshop, the moderator started with a story I knew only too well. My mouth dropped open in surprise as I heard her ask, "Does anyone know the TV show MacGyver?"

Dr. Smiley just grinned at the speaker's ice-breaker, and she leaned over and whispered, "I guess a good story has wings of its own."

As I look back on that day thirty years ago, I'm grateful there were no social media sites. My story would have gone viral in minutes. In fact, I probably would have been the one to post it.

49

Strange Cravings

Bonnie had been a patient in our dental office for years. We watched this young, vibrant woman's health deteriorate due to kidney disease. Her fate was in God's hands. Unfortunately, her life depended on her ranking and status on the organ donor transplant list.

Despite their eagerness to help, none of her family members was a match. Finally, after years of dialysis, a phone call came to inform Bonnie that an organ donor from a fatal accident was a match.

We were all overjoyed that she would soon be on the road to recovery but sad that someone had lost a life. As an office, we felt like she had become family, so we created a meal train and took turns cleaning her home. Bonnie touched our hearts, and we wanted to give back in any way we could.

Bonnie's body accepted the kidney. When she regained her strength, she began sharing her touching story with church and civic groups to raise awareness and advocate for the organ donor program.

As is protocol, privacy laws protect patients and donor families, safeguarding their identity. Therefore, they do not meet unless there is a mutual agreement. A few years after her transplant, Bonnie decided she would like to meet the family who had given her such a precious gift. She learned the organ donor was a paratrooper who died in a military training accident, and the soldier's family was ready to meet the recipient. Soon after, they were in contact with each other.

The Olympic-style "Transplant Games of America" are held annually. Each year a different city hosts the event, this particular year, they were near the soldier's home.

Bonnie, her husband, and two daughters flew from Rochester, NY, to the West Coast to meet the donor's family. Knowing the donor left behind his wife, Joan, and two small children, Bonnie tried to find the right words to thank them for this life-changing gift. Realizing there were no adequate words to express her gratitude, Bonnie embraced the wife in a bear hug, and together they sobbed.

They exchanged stories. The soldier's widow commented that her husband was stationed in Western New York before their marriage. Joan said through her tears, "While he was there, he discovered a local brand of hot dog with an unusual name, *Zweigle's*. He couldn't get enough of them."

Bonnie smiled as she heard the brand.

Bonnie was astonished. "This new information might solve the mystery that has perplexed me since the transplant. I had a strong dislike for the taste and texture of hotdogs."

"Had?" asked Joan.

Bonnie chuckled, "I did some research and found that medically, no one can explain this strange phenomenon, but sometimes transplant recipients crave foods that were favorites of the donor. So your husband's love of *Zweigle's* lives on because now I love them."

The Olympics went well, and Bonnie ran her marathon. Their families bonded in a strong, new friendship; tears of joy and sorrow fell freely. Together, they prayed, thankful for this remarkable experienced.

We are pleased that Bonnie is now healthy. She's thriving and enjoying her role as a wife and mother. Her smile is brighter and happier than ever, and she's forever grateful for the hotdog-loving soldier's incredible gift.

50

The Novice Chef

The hardest part of being a hygienist is trying to clean someone's teeth when they don't stop talking; Carol is one of those patients. When she came in for her appointment, I seated her in my dental chair and turned to reach for the blood pressure cuff. It was the perfect opportunity to roll my eyes without her seeing. I knew this was going to be a long-winded story.

She began, "Oh, Terry, it has been crazy the last six months since Bruce retired. I have to tell you about my husband's newest hobby in my brand new kitchen."

I faced her, smiling, "Well, of course, Carol start from the beginning."

"Bruce decided that since he had so much time on his hands, he wanted to help me by preparing meals. At first, I thought it was great, but it turned out to be such a bad idea."

"Gee, I wish my husband would help," I interjected.

"Oh, no, you don't!" Carol exclaimed. "Bruce decided to take over the grocery shopping, meal planning, and cooking."

"How could that be a bad thing?" I asked.

"Well, for instance, my grocery bills have never been higher."

She explained that Bruce started looking up recipes and is now obsessed with watching YouTube cooking shows. "He was so proud of the first dinner he cooked. I must admit it was delicious, and I was impressed that he served me in the dining room with a perfectly set table."

Carol continued, "I offered to clear the dishes and shrieked when I entered the kitchen. I saw the sink piled high and realized he managed to use every pot, pan, and dish in the cupboards. I looked over to see him dozing on the sofa. He jumped a mile when I shouted, 'Bruce, you cook, then you clean.'"

Carol admitted that after setting the ground rules, things got better. Bruce found a video showing shortcuts in the kitchen that he felt might be helpful. Then, he came upon a demonstration showing how you can take a head of iceberg lettuce and rap it on a counter. Viola, the core will release. He was so excited.

As he rushed to the grocery store, he mumbled, "I have to try that technique. Carol will be impressed."

Bruce reached the produce department and was overwhelmed by the variety of heads of lettuce. Carol explained that just like men never ask for directions, Bruce would never dream of asking for help. He mistook cabbage for lettuce. Anything that grew in a head looked the same to him, so he grabbed one and headed home.

Bruce set the groceries on the counter and grabbed a rather large cabbage from the bag. Beaming, he said, "Let me show you a trick I learned."

Carol told me, "Before I could say a thing, Bruce slammed the cabbage on my new marble counter top making a loud thud. A huge crack appeared. Bruce had a look of horror as his face became pale. I screamed."

Bruce stuttered, "I did it exactly the way they demonstrated on YouTube!"

She told Bruce that she used that technique herself. She then shouted, "You bought cabbage, not lettuce! It makes a big difference!"

I felt awful for Carol. I knew another new counter was going to be costly. She told me Bruce is banned from her kitchen forever. Smiling, I nodded in agreement as Carol added one more detail. "His retirement is not working for me, so I gave him an ultimatum. Bruce has to find a new hobby, or better yet, a new job."

.

51

Sweet Tooth

Amy brought her six-year-old daughter Lucy to her dental appointment. Lucy bounced into the dental chair. She was always enthusiastic to see Mr. Thirsty, our pet name for the saliva suction hose with the spiral-shaped tip. It makes for a pleasant visit when we have cute names for our equipment.

Ron, Amy's husband, has a pest control business. A clever sign on Ron's van attracts attention. In bold letters, it reads: "Hired Killer," with a phone number underneath the tagline. It grabs your attention enough to give it a second glance. In smaller type, the sign proclaims, "We shoot bugs dead! Extermination by Ron."

Lucy asked, "Please can I hold Mr. Thirsty?"

I answered this delightful child with a smile. "Mr. Thirsty has been waiting for you."

Amy started to tell me the newest adventure in their home, and Lucy chimed in before Amy could get another word out of her mouth.

"We had a mouse in the house, and Daddy couldn't catch it!"

Amy laughed, "That doesn't say much for my husband, the exterminator."

I shared in the laughter and listened to the story. This mouse eluded capture for two weeks. There were droppings and evidence of mouse damage in the pantry, under the stove and sink, on counters, and in the closets. It was unmistakable the mouse made its presence known in every room.

 Lucy said, "Mousey ran into my room, and I was scared it would get in my bed."

Amy told me her husband was beyond frustrated because even as a master of his craft, this pesky critter seemed to be winning the cat-and-mouse game. She described Lucy with her big brown eyes filled with tears, asking her daddy. "Daddy, why can't you catch one little mousey?"

Ron was reaching his breaking point, but the mouse made a big mistake last night. It was 2:30 a.m. Amy awoke to her husband stomping around the bedroom.

"What are you doing?" she asked in a groggy tone.

Running around the house in his boxer shorts, Ron yelled, "This is the last straw!"

"Shhhh, you'll wake Lucy!" Amy mumbled.

Amy told me she heard this crackle and crinkle of rustling cellophane paper. Wondering what that was, Amy chuckled as she realized the mouse had found Ron's private stash of his favorite chocolates. She described the mouse pulling a huge Lindor truffle candy across the bedroom floor, still in its bright red wrapper.

"How dare that varmint eat my candy!" Ron shouted.

Amy found it hard to control her laughter. "Ron was determined that night would be the demise of that pesky mouse. Fortunately, dragging the big piece of candy slowed down the critter, so Ron trapped him inside a bedside trash can just as sleepy-eyed Lucy peered into the bedroom. Ron was victorious in catching the mouse but had to promise Lucy he would take mousey far away to find a new home."

Still chuckling, Amy told me, "That mouse didn't bother Ron until his candy was in jeopardy. After that, I didn't get much sleep cause I giggled each time I thought about that determined mouse tugging his prize, not the least bit afraid of the crazed man stomping around the room."

I laughed with Lucy and Amy. "I'll have to tease Ron about his chocolate-loving mouse, but I promise not to spread the story around. It might be bad for business."

52

Unusual Art Gallery

You only have one chance to make a first impression, and Brutus's negative vibes were bone-chilling. About thirty-five years old, with a greasy shoulder-length ponytail, he wore torn jeans and a stained tank top revealing his tattoo sleeves.

Both ears had holes the size of quarters rimmed with purple circles that matched the streak in his hair. A ring hung from the piercing in his nose, and both eyebrows had small straight rods protruding from them. I had no doubt there would also be a tongue piercing when he opened his mouth. My suspicions were correct.

I never clean a patient's teeth with the tongue piercing in place. It's too easy to catch an instrument on it and cause pain or harm to the person or me. So I politely asked Brutus to remove the one-inch long stainless steel rod from the center of his tongue.

Brutus said, "I've never taken this out, so it might be tricky."

It took Brutus a while to unscrew the silver ball that fastened the rod. The metal was slippery, and access from under his tongue was challenging. At last, with this item in soaking mouthwash, I reclined the chair. As I began my exam, the first thing I noticed was the patient's front teeth were chipped from this jewelry.

Now, I was ready to continue my initial exam and dreading what I would find. I was sure every tooth would be in disrepair with rampant decay and teeth beyond saving. This charting would be time-consuming if I had to keep switching from the patient's mouth to a chart and document, so I asked a dental assistant to chart for me.

I was unprepared for what I discovered when Brutus opened his mouth. His oral hygiene was immaculate, and his mouth pristine. The gums were healthy, and when I swept my mirror around his mouth, I discovered a beautiful art gallery.

Amused at my expression, Brutus chuckled, "My friend is an artist and a dental technician. He combined his passions to create these for me."

I was speechless. Upon examination, I found a crown with a yellow sunflower and another with a peace sign fired into the porcelain. The artwork in the mouth faced inside, so the only ones who could see it were dental professionals or Brutus when he was brushing his teeth.

Brutus commented, "I love the one with the red heart, but my friend forgot it was an upper tooth when he was making the crown, so the heart is upside down."

I answered, "I have to say I've never seen colorful images fired into the porcelain. You might be starting a new trend."

After letting her look at the unusual dental work, I dismissed the dental assistant because Brutus needed nothing but a cleaning and the chips on his front teeth smoothed and shaped.

When he left the office, I thought *never judge a book by its cover!*

53

Prizefighter

Like all brides, Sharon, my coworker's daughter, wanted a storybook wedding. She envisioned the perfect wedding day.

Her girlfriends were throwing her bridal shower in New York City. It was the perfect opportunity for her fiancé, Peter, to meet extended family. The engaged couple boarded the subway. Just as the doors were about to close, a man with a knife shoved Sharon and grabbed her purse. Peter jumped from the train and sprinted after the thug. Sharon followed, but she feared for her fiancé's life as they both gave chase.

Peter pounced on the assailant, slamming him to the ground, but not before the kid landed some well-connected punches. Sharon screamed. An undercover cop patrolling the subway station grabbed the hoodlum.

Blood was gushing down Peter's face while his eyes turned majestic shades of green and purple. A trip to the emergency room diagnosed a dislocated nose. Sharon was horrified. She was thankful Peter was safe, but her dream groom looked like a prize fighter who lost the heavyweight division.

Their wedding was only a week away, and Sharon was distraught. There was no possibility his face would be back to normal by the ceremony. "Our wedding was supposed to be sophisticated," she moaned.

Planning took months using the ideas stored in her mind for half a century. Joy, a member of our dental staff, would sing with angelic tones, accompanied by a renowned pianist from the Eastman School of Music, where Sharon had studied years ago.

The bride chose an elegant form-fitting white wedding gown cinched at the waist. Beautifully embellished with pearls, embroidered flowers covered the lace bodice. Her matron of honor chose a peach chiffon sheath. Sharon was thrilled to find a white dress with a peach sash for her niece, the flower girl.

Peter was sorry he made such a mess of things. Sharon tried not to be petty, but she was so upset. She sighed, "He's my hero! I hate that the bruises, which are a tribute to his bravery in protecting me from harm, will ruin our wedding photos."

Peter had a splendid idea three days before the wedding that might save the day. Years ago, Peter had befriended a makeup artist who worked on Broadway. He still had his number. Peter reached out to his friend and pleaded, "It would be a fantastic surprise for my bride and an incredible relief for me if you could help."

As the bride approached the altar on her father's arm, her jaw dropped. Peter's face looked perfect! His steel-blue eyes met hers. Expertly applied stage makeup disguised his bruises so there was no hint of the sickening green hues.

Sharon's eyes sparkled, and her smile grew. Happily, the wedding was just the perfect day she had always dreamed about, with the added bonus of having quite the story to tell.

54

Out of the Mouth of Babes

Kristin brought her young son, Jonah, to her dental appointment. I noticed a cast on his foot. He proudly pointed to his plaster cast and said, "Look, I have a castle on my foot."

I laughed and agreed that it was a beautiful "castle." Then, Jonah proudly announced, "I'm going to have a baby brother!"

The very pregnant mom told me, "Jonah has been picking out names for two years in case he has a baby brother someday. His first choice was Jackson French Fry. If you don't like that one, he has others. The next name he wanted was Tuff, after some wrestler, with a middle name Enuff."

"Cute," I smiled.

I congratulated Jonah and smiled at Kristin, who told me what happened when she found out she was pregnant.

She began, "As any mother will tell you, once you have a child, even a moment of privacy in the bathroom is impossible. I happened to have that snippet of time long enough for me to take a pregnancy test. Jonah barged into the bathroom as I placed the indicator stick on the counter."

"Mommy, what's ya doing? Mommy, what's that? Can I hold it, Mommy?"

Kristin told me she watched as the pregnancy test turned to a plus sign. She was elated. Unable to conceal her joy, she embraced Jonah in a giant bear hug.

"Mommy, you're squishing me!"

"I'm sorry, Jonah, I just love you so much, and Mommy is very happy."

"This stick tells me that you are going to be a big brother!"

Jonah began whooping, hollering, and running in circles, chanting, "I'm gonna be a big brother. I'm gonna be a big brother."

Kristin took in the scene wishing her husband was home to see Jonah's excited reaction.

Without a second thought, Kristin tossed the stick into the trash as she exited the bathroom. Jonah watched in horror. He started screaming. Crying crocodile tears, he was inconsolable. Kristin was confused and tried to comfort Jonah to no avail. Embracing him again, the flustered mother pleaded. "What's the matter, Jonah? Tell Mommy, why are you crying?"

Jonah's chin quivered. His shoulders shook as sobs racked his tiny body. He was tugging at his hair and moaning.

Again Kristin tried to find out what took this little boy from ecstatic to so dramatic. "Jonah, honey, how can Mommy help? Why are you so upset? Show Mommy."

Breaking away from the hug, Jonah kept pointing to the trash can. Violently shaking his finger, still pointing, he dove into the receptacle to retrieve the pregnancy test.

He screamed in an anguished voice, uncharacteristic of a four-year-old. "Mommy, pleeease, Mommy, don't throw my little brother away!"

Kristin looked at him in disbelief and confusion. A huge grin came over her face as she realized he had equated the pregnancy test with his new sibling. Calmly, she retrieved the test stick and placed it in a plastic bag where it would remain until his little brother was born.

55

The Petting Zoo Caper

Sandra arrived at the dental office smelling funky, putting it politely. She apologized that she didn't have time to go home to shower. As the executive director of a camp for children with special needs, she usually dressed in business attire for her appointment. I said, "I'm curious about the random pieces of hay in your hair."

"I apologize for being such a mess," she began. "A farmer donated two docile, pygmy goats for the camp petting zoo but couldn't transport them. I offered to get them. I just got back and came straight to the appointment with you. Sorry."

She explained that she took her program director, Mandy, and a borrowed cargo van to make the forty-mile trip to pick up the promised pygmy goats. Sandra was excited to introduce the campers to the adorable animals she knew the children would love.

When they arrived at the farm, it appeared there was some misunderstanding because the goats were large and aggressive. *"Not a good match for a petting zoo,"* Mandy thought. Confused and disappointed, Mandy had no choice but to take the donated goats she had already agreed to accept.

Sandra sighed, "I had no idea the farmer decided to switch out the goats without telling us."

Mandy said, "I overheard the farmer tell his wife he sold the pygmy goats to the yoga studio for goat yoga. Have you ever heard of such a thing?"

Coaxing reluctant full-sized goats to go up a ramp into the van required a clever strategy. Sandra realized she should have had cages for the animals to protect them during transport. Worse yet, there was no division between the driver and passengers from the animals. After tying ropes around the neck of each goat, enticing them with a fresh scoop of hay, pushing and pulling, they loaded the stubborn animals, then quickly closed the van doors.

She continued, "We immediately noticed the goats didn't like each other. They jockeyed for position near the front of the vehicle, near us. Butting heads, the goats turned their aggression to the van's side panels that dented easily. They relieved themselves multiple times, and soon the van began to reek. We could barely breathe!"

Sandra told me she was driving with Mandy riding shotgun. "Each of us felt the goats nibbling at our hair. We tried swatting at the livestock, but it didn't help. I almost had an accident when one goat grabbed my hair and jerked my head back. He yanked a huge wad of hair off my head. I got the van under control, but the jolt caused me to bite my tongue. You will surely see the welt when you clean my teeth."

If that wasn't bad enough, the goats made ear-piercing bleating noises and loud snorts as they chewed everything in sight, including the upholstery. Suddenly the skies opened up, and torrential rain made driving even more difficult. The forty-mile drive felt more like a hundred as the wretched stench proved to be unnerving, and now they had to close the windows. The women were at their wit's end, wondering how they would ever explain what happened.

Sandra said, "All I could think of was how impossible it will be to clean and deodorize this vehicle, not to mention what it would cost to repair the upholstery."

Sandra and Mandy looked at each other as they approached the children's camp, imagining the horror scene that was about to unravel. The goats hadn't settled down the entire trip, and the women realized the potential danger. They were terrified these crazed goats would frighten the children, causing nightmares, or worse, yet injure one of them.

As they pulled into the campgrounds to deliver the wild cargo, they knew they couldn't let the children near these monsters. The rain stopped by then, and a magnificent double rainbow appeared. The campers poured out of their cabins to see the glorious colors in the sky. Mandy hoped they could sneak in unnoticed and unload the destructive critters with no one around.

Someone hollered, "The goats are here!" Dozens of campers in wheelchairs spun around from looking at the rainbow and moved forward to the petting zoo area. The campers cheered while Sandra and Mandy cringed.

Surprisingly, the goats eagerly trotted down the ramp out of the destroyed van. Then, something remarkable happened as the beasts seemed to be reveling in the attention the audience of boisterous children was giving them. Sandra didn't trust these creatures, but the goats seemed to come alive with brand-new personalities as the campers neared. With gentle bleating sounds, the goats romped about, coming near the fence, begging to be petted and eating the food pellets the youngsters clutched in their little hands. Thankfully, the newest members of the petting zoo seemed to mellow and be fascinated by all the smiling children.

Sandra related that she rubbed the bald spot on her head and asked Mandy, "What happened to the demon goats that were in the back of the van?"

As we finished chatting and I prepared to clean Sandra's teeth, one of the office dental assistants gently closed the door to my treatment room while holding her nose as Sandra was telling me this was not the first time she had witnessed the transformative power of the love of a child.

56

Bearing It All

It had been a nerve-wracking start to the day. One of our co-workers, Sophia, wasn't feeling well. My boss realized that Sophia was experiencing symptoms of what could be signs of a significant cardiac event. We weren't taking any chances, so we called 911.

Our dental office, located in a rural community, is serviced by a volunteer fire department. We did have to chuckle when a paramedic, who was plowing nearby, pulled up on his huge tractor. No matter his mode of transportation, we were grateful he was there. The office was full of patients, and our EMT greeted everyone by name, including his uncle Bill, in one of the dental chairs. Soon the ambulance arrived, and they whisked Sophia off to the hospital.

We tried to continue as if nothing had happened, but it was nearly impossible until we heard Sophia was stable and kept for observation. My nerves were just starting to calm down when my next patient arrived. With all the commotion, I hadn't checked the day's schedule. Inwardly, I groaned.

Sasha was a nice enough woman, but her fear of dentistry and jumpy twitches made her a difficult patient. She arrived in her bib overalls, reeking of hay and horse manure. I gagged at the pungent odor as I led her to my treatment room. My eyes widened with surprise when she stripped down to her underwear, leaving her coveralls in a heap on the floor. I was speechless!

"I just finished mucking the horse stalls. I only had time to change my boots," Sasha grumbled.

Watching in disbelief as she was ready to pull her t-shirt over her head, I was quick to comment, "Wait, you can leave that on!"

Coaxing her into my dental chair was no easy feat. I kept a blanket handy for patients who were cold and handed it to her. I never imagined it would be used for a patient in her underwear. Thankfully she covered herself, but whenever I tried to get her to open her mouth, she'd put her hand up. "Wait, please wait. I have to prepare myself mentally!"

Since I was unsuccessful in beginning my dental exam, I said, "Sasha, remember the relaxation techniques we discussed at your last visit? You promised me you'd practice those before you got here today."

Sasha was always a problematic patient, and it was difficult to stay professional. "Do you want the headphones to listen to your favorite music?"

She agreed, and I reclined the chair, picked up my instruments, and began my oral exam. Just as I predicted, she started fidgeting. I was trying to concentrate when I was startled by a sharp noise. I jumped and dropped the mouth mirror.

"Was that a bark coming from your purse?" I asked.

Sasha bounced out of the chair and made a beeline for her handbag. She pulled out a pint-sized dog, got back in the dental chair, and placed the dog on her chest with its head under her chin. She said, "Okay-I'm all set. You can work now."

I looked at her as the dog snarled, bearing his teeth. My hygiene assistant and I looked at each other in disbelief.

"Sasha, I can't possibly clean your teeth with that dog ready to attack me!" I said. "Dogs aren't even allowed in the office."

She got up with a huff, and as she stormed out of the treatment room, I handed her the mound of smelly clothes. "You might need these," I said, gladly sending her on her merry way.

57

Barnyard Dentistry

After working for decades in a dental office, I thought nothing could surprise me. I was mistaken!

Betty was an eccentric person, to say the least. She was always complaining and uncomfortable. Even the simplest procedures we performed made her complain. So we finally began offering nitrous oxide (laughing gas) to help her relax.

I said, "Betty, the doctor would like you to be comfortable so we won't charge extra."

Betty was now happy, and we didn't let on that we never charged extra for using the gas. It made her feel special and helped us complete our dental services without frequent squirming in the chair.

I explained, "This next appointment is going to be rather complicated and lengthy." Before I could say another word, Betty announced she would need to bring her service animal to calm her. I knew refusing entry for a service animal was illegal, so I reluctantly agreed.

We prepared the treatment room and waited for our patient's arrival with her service animal. Betty strolled into the dental office with Ginger, a potbellied pig, on a leash.

In a panic, the receptionist ran to Dr. Smiley's office, talking faster than anyone could understand. With her arms flailing, the receptionist blurted out, "You won't believe it! You just won't believe it!"

I laughed, envisioning a cute, cuddly little creature we picture when we hear potbellied pig. "It can't be that bad," I exclaimed. "Betty told me the animal sits on her lap and cuddles."

"Really?" the receptionist exclaimed.

With Ginger on a pink leash, Betty made her way to the treatment room. My mouth dropped open when I spotted the animal. Before me, I saw a full-grown, one-hundred-and-fifty-pound pig grunting and knocking over equipment.

It was quite a conundrum. As Betty seated herself, we had no idea how we could accommodate such a huge, unruly animal in the treatment area. Ginger, the pig, rested her snout on Betty's lap. We needed to figure out the health codes in such an impossible situation.

Our dilemma was soon solved when I asked for the papers verifying that Ginger was a trained service animal. Betty confessed her pet had no formal instruction and was not certified, but she pleaded for the pig to stay since the animal soothed her anxiety.

My mask hid my exasperated expression. I thought *Ginger might calm Betty's anxiety, but it's sending mine through the roof.*

I politely asked Betty to leave before the cute piglet left us a present on the carpet. We escorted the duo out a side door before any patients got wind of our barnyard friend.

Unintentionally, the receptionist planned this appointment well, having scheduled Betty as the last patient before the lunch break. It proved to be a lifesaver. When the patient left, massive amounts of Lysol spray filled the treatment room, and every surface was scrubbed and disinfected.

With combined effort, we were able to have the office ready for the afternoon patients. We all laughed when our first patient after lunch was holding a toy playing "Old McDonald Had a Farm." I looked at the little girl, giggled, and sang along, "E-i-e-i-o."

58

Holiday Treats

The holidays were over; this was my first day back to work. Donna sat in my dental chair, and I asked her, "How was your Christmas?"

"Wonderful!" she answered. "The twins were home from college, and my son drove in from Raleigh. My husband, Jack, and I were excited to have them all together."

"I know how great that feels," I said.

At a previous appointment, Donna shared that her aging dog, Milo, had become a very picky eater.

I asked, "How's your dog?"

Donna laughed and said he was the hit of Christmas morning. She told me that her friend's daughter opened a new bakery specializing in gourmet dog treats. "I guess I got carried away and spent forty dollars on dog cookies."

"Wow, that's one lucky pooch!"

Donna continued, "Christmas morning, since the excitement of opening presents with little ones is gone, Jack encouraged Milo as he sniffed his packages and tore them open." We laughed as he kept asking, "Milo, what did you get for Christmas?

"I can just picture it," I chuckled.

Donna giggled as she said, "When Milo finished tearing the presents, I let him eat a few treats and then repacked what remained in the colorful box from the store. The tin, decorated with different breeds of dogs, had the shop's name in bold embossed letters. I told my friend what a great business her daughter had opened."

"I don't have a dog, but I'll pass on the referral to patients." I cheerfully added.

"You'll love this," Donna said. "I came home from work yesterday. Milo greeted me as I opened the treat box, wagging his tail enthusiastically. The container was empty. I became upset knowing my dog would get sick if he ate too many at one time."

My husband saw me with the tin and said, "Donna, those were the worst cookies I've ever tasted. I almost broke a tooth, so I just threw them out."

Donna told me she snorted and couldn't contain her laughter. "Jack, those were for the dog! You saw Milo opening the cookies on Christmas. Didn't you read the box? Didn't you see that each cellophane-wrapped treat was shaped like a bone and had a tag reading *Off the Leash Barkery?*"

"That's a great story, Donna. I know the kids will never let him live that one down," I smiled. "What did Jack do?"

"He started gagging and ran into the bathroom to brush his teeth while the kids and I couldn't stop laughing."

59

Things that Go Boom in the Night

Madeline came to the dental office with bloodshot eyes. She explained she had just returned from a trip to Brazil and was still jet-lagged. I told her she could close her eyes while I cleaned her teeth, but she started sharing many details about the trip. Finally, I put down my instruments and listened to her story.

She began, "Who knew there are twenty million people in São Paulo? I was unprepared for this huge city and amazed when we toured their version of Hollywood, complete with a Rodeo Drive shopping area. It was a far cry from the jungle life I had pictured."

Madeline continued. "After a full day of activity, I returned to the hotel and settled in for the night. I always have trouble sleeping in a strange bed, but thankfully I nodded off. I awoke with a start as a loud banging noise began at 2:30 a.m. My heart was pounding. It scared me to death."

She told me that, at first, she thought someone was trying to break into the room. "I even jumped out of bed to look out the window to see if it was some kind of Brazilian Carnivale celebration or fireworks as the deafening thumpity-thump-thump-boom-boom racket continued."

The banging finally stopped, only to start again. Madeline realized the noise would come through the sprinkler heads when the air-conditioning kicked on. "That was it for any more sleep that night," she said with a groan. Madeline wondered how to explain the problem to the Portuguese-speaking Concierge when an idea formed. Madeline took out her cell phone and recorded the racket. "Thank heaven for today's technology," she thought.

She managed to get across that there was a problem in her room. She pulled out the cell phone and showed the hotel employee the video as the loud banging rang out. Madeline, using hand gestures and a few words of Portuguese, explained that she would be out all day and would appreciate the matter resolved.

The Concierge nodded, apologetic, but laughed as he said in broken English. "Ahhhh, noise. Not fixed? I sorry."

Upon arriving back at the hotel, Madeline checked the room. It sounded quiet. She went to bed, but the continuous noise started all over again at 2:30. Exasperated, she rolled over. After another sleepless night, Madeline arose and turned on the shower. As she lathered her hair, she felt water pooling around her ankles. Rinsing the shampoo from her eyes and looking down, she whispered to herself. "I took a shower here yesterday. What seems to be the problem today?"

It wasn't easy to see through the soapy water. Madeline surmised that the drain seemed plugged. Then, turning off the water, and groping on her hands and knee, feeling no holes, only a solid metal plate, "What is going on?" she wondered.

She was freezing but kept feeling around the center of the shower. Madeline played with the drain for a long time until she found a lever that could slide to unplug the holes. As the water began to recede, Madeline realized the shower had no lip, just a door and flat surface level with the bathroom floor. She toweled off, waiting for the water to empty. She didn't dare open the shower door for fear of flooding the entire bathroom until the last swoosh of water went down the drain bathroom.

Her plan didn't work because she stepped out of the shower into another puddle of four inches of water. Then, with her towel wrapped around her, she grabbed every remaining towel in the bathroom to mop up the water.

Madeline opened the door to the bedroom, confident that the water disaster was behind her. But, to her astonishment, the bedroom was flooded. The carpet was soaked. It squished and sloshed, splashing her as she walked. "What a nightmare," she cried out.

Madeline was so grateful her luggage was on a rack off the floor. She dressed and returned to the same concierge desk attended by the same man she had visited just yesterday. Shyly, she began. "Umm-hi-it's me again," She showed him the video again and said, "Not fixed, and by the way, I flooded the bathroom and bedroom."

In his politest broken English, the Concierge said, "Would you like another room?" She nodded. "Problem solved," She thought.

Later that evening, Madeline met friends in the hotel lobby. She laughed as she told the story of the things that go boom in the night. Showing them the video, Madeline said, "I recorded this because I didn't know how I was going to explain to the hotel staff about the noise, and then today I had to explain the flood."

"They gave me a new room," she continued.

"Really, what room were you in?' Ralph, a co-worker, asked.

"Four-eleven," she answered.

"Great minds think alike," Ralph said as he pulled out his phone and played a video of the exact same boom-boom sound he heard in his room three-eleven, directly below. "It was an awful racket that kept me awake for two nights," Ralph complained.

As they chatted, Ralph played a second video for the group. Madeline's eyes became huge as she watched in disbelief. It showed water pouring from the ceiling fixture over his bed. Ralph exclaimed, "Good thing I reached for the phone because the plaster came crashing on the bed right where my head had been."

"Was he alright?" I asked.

Madeline added, smiling, "I gasped when I realized the seriousness, and he could have injuries. Thankfully, he wasn't hurt."

In unison, Ralph and Madeline said, "I guess we'll both be getting new rooms."

With a smile, Ralph added, "Not exactly the luxury hotel we expected; maybe we should change hotels, not just rooms."

60

Ghostly Encounters

The new dental assistant, Audrey, was a great addition to our office staff. She and her husband, Daniel, recently purchased an old working farm in Pennsylvania as a vacation home. They negotiated an incredibly meager price since locals believed ghosts occupied the dwelling.

My husband, Harry, and I enjoyed the beautiful countryside and rolling hills on our three-hour drive to their farm. Our friends greeted us, and the grand tour began. Just as Harry was going to mention a spongy section of floor, the boards gave way, wedging his foot into ankle-deep water in the ten-inch crawl space. My husband commented, "It would be a real money pit if you tried to fix this place up. You'd be better off starting from scratch. Maybe you can salvage some old wood doors and that great mantel."

Daniel said, "I hope you're not squeamish, but there are a lot of ghost stories associated with this one-hundred–fifty-year-old house. Unfortunately, the neighbors have been hesitant to give details of these ghostly tales but swear it's undeniable that this property is haunted."

Audrey told us, "The first day we were here, the ghost made himself known. I'm certain he made sure we were both present because I think neither of us would have believed the other. In a muffled but distinct voice, the ghost said, 'H-e-l-l-o.' The accent was unique and typical for this part of Pennsylvania."

Audrey wrapped her arms in a self-hugging fashion. "I was shivering and ready to bolt from the house, but I nervously said, 'H-e-l-l-o!' My husband was a little calmer, but in a shaky voice, thanked the ghost for the wonderful farm."

Daniel explained, "We think the ghost is a Civil War soldier whose family owned the property. We tend to see at least one ghost sighting each time we come here. Typically, a large shadow crosses the room or a door slams, accompanied by the distinct sound of footsteps."

I stood motionless as the floor creaked, and then I leaped towards Harry as a door slammed. With my heart pounding, I declared, "The hairs are standing up on the back of my neck. I pray your ghost likes strangers,"

Daniel laughed. "We're used to it. We are considering tearing down this farmhouse but don't want retaliation from the ghost. What do you think?"

In a joking tone, Harry said, "You definitely don't want to enrage your resident spirit, so why don't you ask him if it's okay."

As we drove home, I told Harry, "I'm so glad we didn't accept their invitation to spend the night. I'd be afraid to sleep inside!" Harry just smiled and continued driving.

In my bedroom at home, a loud voice awakened me two nights after visiting the farm. It was 4:00 a.m., and I jolted into a sitting position in bed. My heart was pounding. I looked around, but it was too dark to see anything. Was I dreaming?

Did a dream wake me, or did I hear a voice? My husband was sound asleep, so he was no help. I was sure it was a man's deep voice, and I thought I heard something about a meteor. I rationalized that I was overthinking about these ghosts. Sleep eluded me for the rest of the night.

Two nights later, I bolted awake at 2:00 a.m. In a sleepy haze, I heard "meteor" and then "danger, hazard, and threat."

I was overcome with fear as I became fully awake. I knew it was a distinctive voice, not a dream. I was scared. "Okay, what is going on?" I said aloud. I gripped Harry's arm so tight that my knuckles were white. It did the trick to wake him up.

"Are you crazy? What are you doing? That hurts!" He was practically shouting. I told him about the strange voice. Harry groaned, rolled over, and fell back asleep.

At work, I confessed to Audrey that I was hearing voices in the night.

"Does your ghost ever say anything besides hello?" I asked.

In a reassuring tone, she said, "Don't be silly. There's no reason for you to have ghosts."

"Maybe they followed me back." I shuddered as I said the words aloud. "Enough ghost talk. I'm going to forget about it. I should seat my next patient."

My mind was still whirling, with visions of ghosts floating around my bedroom. It was a puzzling mystery, and I was trying to compile the clues. Then, a few nights later, while I was in a blissful state of deep sleep, I was startled by a piercing, shrilling, whistling noise followed by a man's voice. This time my husband bolted upright.

"What in the world is that?" he demanded.

"You heard it too?"

We were wide awake. I knew this wasn't a dream. We both understood a man's voice loud and clear. I started to tremble. That's when I heard the deep voice say, "Danger, a threat of frost warning during the night, a report from our meteorologist of the Weather Channel."

I looked at my nightstand, and my cell phone was vibrating. I couldn't contain myself and burst out laughing. I turned on the lights and said, "Harry, our mystery is solved. It's not a ghost, but the emergency alert on the new weather App I installed on my smartphone. Let's get some sleep."

61

Things are Not Always as They Seem

Ron always drove his Harley in good weather, and I heard its roar entering the parking lot. I thought Ron would enjoy the story of the crazy three-wheeled motorcycle driver I saw yesterday.

I began, "A rather large woman in a pink helmet was doing everything except having her hands on the controls of her bike. Her erratic driving seemed very dangerous, so I dropped back. I laughed when I was directly behind her because it was an illusion. She was, in reality, the passenger, blocking my view of the driver."

Laughing, I told Ron, "Things are not always as they seem."

Ron chuckled, "You're right! Follow me into the parking lot after my appointment. I have something to show you."

I nodded, "I bet you have a new Harley."

"Kind of," Ron said with a grin.

We continued his appointment, and when I updated his medical chart, Ron told me he had been diagnosed with Multiple Sclerosis.

"The disease was affecting my mobility and fine motor skills. My Harley is my pride and joy, and not being able to ride and feel the wind in my face was taking its toll on me. As a result, I was sinking into a deep depression."

"Ron, I am so sorry," I said sympathetically.

Ron explained, "I was devastated at the thought of giving up my motorcycle, but driving it was no longer an option with my balance issues; a trike motorcycle didn't work either. Fortunately, my very caring and clever neurologist came up with an idea for me to be able to continue riding."

I followed Ron to the parking lot when the appointment was over. I was intrigued. There sat a shiny new Harley with an attached sidecar. I was reasonably confused because I thought Ron came alone.

"Who came with you today?"

Ron pointed to his motorcycle, "No one. I drove here."

"How?" I asked, surprised.

He chuckled at my confused expression. "My doctor talked to a motorcycle dealer. They had an innovative idea but didn't know if it was even possible. So, they contacted a mutual friend who was studying engineering. A custom-designed sidecar was mounted on the Harley using the latest technology available. With hand controls, I can drive this rider-less-motorcycle from the sidecar. It has been incredibly life-altering! I wish you could see the looks I get!"

As I saw Ron pull out onto the road, I saw drivers do double-takes of the tricked-out motorcycle. Even though I knew about the unique modifications, seeing that empty saddle seat as the bike drove down the road was surreal.

As I said earlier, "Things are not always as they seem."

62

A Concrete Adventure

I stepped out into the waiting room, looking for my next patient, only to find Doug had taken his wife's appointment. It would have been nice if they called ahead, but I understood. Doug traveled forty weeks out of the year. He had just flown home due to an unexpected cancellation in his scheduled presentations, giving him the rare opportunity to have a dental appointment.

I seated Doug, and he told me he had been in Boston three weeks ago. "I've been racking up reward points with hotel and car rentals, so the rental agent upgraded me to a Lamborghini. It was a beautiful two-hundred-thousand-dollar car."

"Wow," I remarked.

He continued, "I was enjoying driving that luxury sports car, but the hotel I booked was further from my speaking engagement than I had thought. Since I was giving a significant part of the presentation, I worried about being late. My impatience with the traffic was spoiling my fun."

I listened intently as the rest of the story spilled out. "I was aware of the massive construction project coined the Big Dig, and I knew getting around Boston was a nightmare." He said he was driving on the expressway when he witnessed an accident happening directly in front of him in his lane of traffic. In a relieved tone, he said, "I was far enough back from the multicar pileup that I was able to stop my car, but vehicles around me were swerving, trying to gain control."

Just when he thought he was clear, the car beside him barreled into a cement truck next to him. It looked like the drivers were unhurt, but Doug noticed the chute had dislodged.

"It was like I was in another dimension; events seemed to unfold in slow motion. The chute swung left and right. Then the churning cement truck started to spew its contents all over the expressway. My rental car took a direct hit."

I gasped and said, "Oh, No!"

"I was helpless to do anything but sit in the cement-covered car. I turned on the windshield wipers and was able to get a small hole to peer out to drive. Somehow I was able to get around the mess. I passed a car wash that was closed, so I continued driving and pulled up to the posh hotel where I was giving my speech."

Doug continued, "The valet jumped back to avoid getting splattered by the concrete dropping off my car. He gasped when he noticed the Lamborghini insignia barely visible on the hood. He yelled, 'You can't leave this car with me!'"

I waved him off and yelled back, "I'm the keynote speaker." I tossed him the keys and ran into the hotel.

"Several hours later, the valet brought the expensive car around, completely encased in hardening concrete. It was a miracle the doors opened. I had no time to deal with the problem and drove directly to the airport car rental return. It had an automated return kiosk, and I just left the Lamborghini, hoping for the best. I ran to the gate to catch my flight."

Shaking his head, he said, "Last week, a certified letter came from the car rental agency. Enclosed was a bill with a list of damages totaling twenty thousand dollars."

I responded, "Oh my, what are you going to do?"

"I just chuckled and forwarded it to my boss. I'd love to see the look on his face when he sees the enclosed photo of the car."

"Ok, Doug, it's time to get serious, open wide. Oh my, you need to come to the dentist more often. This stuff on your teeth looks as hard as concrete."

63

Runaway Walker

Darlene had a lot of physical therapy sessions after her car accident. So I was pleased to see her come in for a dental appointment.

She suffered head trauma and extensive damage to her lower limbs. With great determination, strength, and the power of prayer, she could walk with the assistance of a cane or walker. After speaking with her, another side effect was apparent: some fuzzy moments in short-term memory.

Darlene and I chatted as I updated her medical history. She told me she was still getting used to her limited mobility. I commented, "I noticed the sign on your walker."

Darlene said, "After a few embarrassing and complicated incidents, the sign was necessary."

I laughed and said, "That laminated sign with those big, bold letters SET BRAKES should be a pretty good reminder."

We continued with the cleaning appointment, intermittently conversing. Darlene told me that she found herself exhausted last week during a supermarket trip. "Limping, using my cane, I made my way to the car and drove home."

Darlene said, "My walker, which I keep in the car, is one of those fancy ones with a seat that is handy if I have groceries to take into the house. I hooked my cane around the walker and placed my bags on the seat."

"My walker!" she screamed as it careened down the sloped driveway spewing canned goods left and right. "The brake, I never remember to set the brake!"

To her astonishment, Darlene saw the UPS truck run over the shiny red walker and keep going. Exasperated that she had forgotten her cell phone, Darlene grabbed onto the railing along the walkway to make it safely inside, leaving the mess in the street. She sighed, "What a day!"

Darlene continued, "My daughter admonished me, explaining that the incident of the runaway walker was inexcusable." Darlene hung her head and said, "Later that afternoon, my daughter went shopping to buy a new walker and installed this sign on the seat to remind me to set the brake."

"Another time, after leaving a doctor's appointment, I began transferring into the car before my daughter was there to help me. We were concentrating on getting me settled, not noticing the walker rolling into the parking lot."

"My daughter reprimanded me, 'Mom, you have to remember to set the brake!'"

"The next day, I had my toddler-age grandson on the walker seat when I turned to see what his sister was doing, and of course, I never set the brake."

My daughter shrieked, "Mom, grab the walker! Grab Jacob!"

"It was good that the walker was still at arm's length since the path was on an inclining grade. I shudder when I think Jacob could have been hurt," she said in a strained voice.

"That night, my daughter insisted I sign a pledge that reads, 'I, Darlene Lovejoy, promise never to leave the house without my cell phone, and I solemnly promise to always set the break on my walker.'"

I looked at Darlene and said, "You are not off to a good start, my dear. When I moved your walker, I realized you forgot to set the brake. Maybe you need a bigger sign!"

64

Technology to the Rescue

Joan seated herself in my dental chair. Today, perky as ever, this nurse specializing in geriatrics had a great story to share. Last week she got a raise because she solved a mystery that had baffled the doctors in her practice for years.

Joan's primary job was to handle the phones in the morning to triage patients. In addition, she was responsible for offering medical advice and deciding if someone needed an appointment. Predictably, like clockwork, precisely at 9:30 a.m. almost every day, a call would come from a lonely, seventy-five-year-old man named Jeb Wilson.

He always recognized her voice when Joan said hello. He would say the exact words, "Miss Joan, this is Jeb; I haven't pooped yet."

I raised my eyebrows as I listened. Then finally, I snickered, "Are you kidding?"

Other staff members were annoyed by Jeb, but accustomed to this daily routine, dismissing the old gent. Only Joan took time to hear what he was saying between the lines.

She noticed that he only called on the days his bowel movement did not come before 9:30. Her mind filled with questions. What was significant about the time? A good nurse often must play detective and investigate the problem.

After months of these phone calls, Joan prepared for Mr. Wilson. She told her insistent caller, "You know, Mr. Wilson, we'll try something different every day until we conquer this constipation issue. If my recommendations don't work, I'll get you an appointment with the doctor."

Mr. Wilson replied, "I'll try anything, but if I have to come to see the doctor, it has to be after 11:30 a.m. I can't miss my TV show."

Joan stopped in her tracks. "Did I hear him correctly?"

Now subtle little comments he made in the past were beginning to make sense. He calls whenever he doesn't have a bowel movement before 9:30. "Let me get this straight, Mr. Wilson. I must ask you a very important question. Are all these calls about a television program?

"Oh yes, my dear," he replied. "My favorite program comes on at ten, and I just can't miss it."

Joan asked again, "Am I correct that all the concern about not having a bowel movement before 9:30 is because you don't want to miss a game show?"

"Yes, it is!" He answered with a loud chuckle.

Joan was speechless, but a plan started to form in her mind. She asked, "Mr. Wilson do you have an iPad?"

Mr. Wilson retrieved his tablet, and the lesson began. Joan spoke slowly. "Turn it on. Now pull up the internet. Ok, now see if there is a free App for TV. Are you with me so far?"

"Yes, this is fun! My grandson has been a great teacher of this new-fangled device." Mr. Wilson exclaimed.

Joan turned around and could see her co-workers looking puzzled. Then finally, one nurse asked, "Joan, are you triaging an App?"

Joan couldn't answer. She had to focus on the task. They certainly didn't teach this in nursing school.

Concentrating hard, Joan asked, "Mr. Wilson has the App loaded?"

When he said yes, she explained the advantages of having his television program on this device:

1. She told him he could take the iPad into the bathroom and watch it live.
2. She explained that he could watch it anytime on demand.
3. Most importantly, there wasn't any reason for him to miss his program if Mother Nature did not cooperate with his bathroom habit.

Mr. Wilson said, "You're an angel, my dear. Thank you."

Joan explained the story of the television show that Mr. Wilson refused to miss to her boss. The doctor started laughing and couldn't stop. He told her the nurse she replaced had spent more hours than they could count on the phone with Mr. Wilson and his pooping problem. Dr.

Spiller complimented Joan that she realized this was all about a TV show, not a medical issue, after just a few months.

We were both laughing when Joan finished her story. Then, quite matter-of-factly, with an unmistakable charm, Joan said, "I'll never be able to watch *Let's Make a Deal* without picturing Mr. Wilson on the commode."

65

Grannle Bloomers

Patricia had been a dental patient of mine for years. I ran into her a few weeks ago at the mall, and she told me she had been shopping for comfortable travel outfits. We chatted outside a lingerie store. She commented, "My budget is pretty tight, especially with the vacation expenses, but it was time to throw away the granny panties and purchase new underwear."

When Patricia came in for her appointment, she told me she had just returned from her trip. Her grandson, Jake, accompanied her, and she was anxious to tell me about it. I was glad the next patient canceled, so I had extra time.

As she was getting dressed to go to the airport in the wee hours of the morning, Patricia was pleased she purchased the spandex panties that would flatter her figure. However, she was suddenly irritated. She realized she had thrown out all the old underwear but failed to leave a pair of her newly purchased unmentionables with the clothes she had planned to wear. Her suitcase overflowed, and any attempt to open it would be a disaster. Frantically rummaging around her room, she found one lonely pair of dingy, well-worn panties hidden in the back of a drawer.

"Whew," she sighed, donning the old underpants. As she continued to dress, she found the elastic from the panties was unraveling and got stuck in her zipper. It was 3:00

a.m., and it just would have to work. "I'll just throw them out in California," she thought. She finished getting dressed. Patricia grabbed a travel mug of coffee and rushed to the airport with sleepy Jake in tow.

"We arrived at the terminal with not much time to spare. Hurrying to get out the door, I didn't take time to attend to personal needs, and now my coffee was kicking in. We waited in long security lines, and I rushed to a ladies' room. Jake is twelve and too old to enter the ladies' room, but I was nervous leaving him unattended."

Patricia parked Jake right outside the restroom door. She loaded him down with coats and carry-ons. Scurrying, she rushed into the restroom as Jake protested, "But Grandma…"

Patricia cut him off, admonishing him. "Just wait here and don't move," she shouted as she entered the restroom. Jake answered with a smirk on his face, "Yes, Grandma."

Patricia was annoyed by his sarcastic tone as she rushed into a stall. Completely repulsed by the condition of the restroom, she refused to use that cubicle. When she turned around, Patricia gasped as she noticed the urinals. Unfortunately, in her haste, she didn't spot the six-foot-high silhouette identifying the men's room.

She gasped as she said, "I darted out of there visibly sweating, rubbing the back of my neck. Jake was standing right where I left him, but he was now snickering. Good thing the restroom was empty, or I would have been mortified."

Jake tried to compose himself as his crazy grandma repeated, "Stay put and don't move a muscle." Finally, she hurried into the proper restroom, thinking, "We will never make that plane."

"Who designs these restrooms?" Patricia said out loud. The stall was tight, and Patricia had to straddle the toilet to close the door. Hurriedly, Patricia placed her purse on the fold-down shelf in the cubicle. Then remembering the zipper jammed, she struggled with the unruly elastic. Patricia was finally successful and sighed. "Whew, relief!"

Grabbing her belongings and pulling up her pants, Patricia was frustrated because the auto-flush mechanism kept engaging and splashing her behind. She headed to the sink to wash her hands, wishing she could take a complete shower.

"I didn't realize the frayed elastic had become entangled in the fold-down shelf hinge. As I walked to the sink, it continued unraveling, following me across the room. Another hurried traveler rushed into the restroom, and I felt a strong tug dragging me backward. The woman bounced back off the seemingly invisible elastic trail blocking her path. We looked at each other, puzzled, until I noticed my elastic tail. You would have thought it was as thick as a bungee cord the way I got pulled back."

Patricia apologized to the confused woman. "I struggled but couldn't rip the elastic to spring free. So, I had to dash back into the stall and leave the undies hanging there while I pulled up my slacks on my bare bottom."

I was laughing as I listened.

"Jake was obediently standing in the exact spot I had left him. He said, stifling a chuckle, 'What's the matter, grandma? Your face is all red.'"

Patricia stammered, "Jake, don't even ask me! No time to explain!"

"But Grandma…" Jake tried to interject.

Frazzled, Patricia admonished Jake, "Shush and hurry. Let's get on the plane. They're boarding."

Jake shrugged as Grandma pushed him ahead. He would have to ignore the wad of toilet paper stuck to Patricia's shoe that trailed behind her like the tail on a kite.

66

The Godiva Night

Working part-time in two offices had been fun and a great blessing. Dr. Smiley and her staff gave me a great sendoff with a party and luscious dinner at my favorite restaurant. The gift of airline vouchers and a memory scrapbook signed by many of the patients brought me to tears. I had been with her for fourteen years, and goodbyes are always difficult. Now, I had to do the same with Dr. Richards and his employees I worked with for twenty-five years.

You may remember my boss, Dr. Richards. He stayed behind when he sent his wife and the dental office staff on fabulous, all-expenses-paid trips. Our travels took us to Hawaii, Ireland, France, and Canada, to name a few of our awe-inspiring destinations.

It was May of 2005. We were off to explore another fabulous location. This journey was incredibly bittersweet for me since I was moving out of state the following week. Sadly, this was my last trip with these great friends.

Our itinerary took us to Charleston, South Carolina. We stayed in a private cottage in the historic district at a charming B & B, The Palmer House. We were curious why it was painted pink. On our first carriage tour, as we passed the "Pink Lady," the driver answered our question. We learned the original owner was a dentist who wanted to remind everyone to have a healthy mouth, so he painted the house pink. We laughed at the irony of staying in the "house of healthy gums."

As I feared, our time together was coming to an end. We had one more place to explore on our last evening. Ruth chose to stay behind and urged us to go, calling out, "Have a memorable evening."

We strolled down the sidewalk to a rooftop restaurant in Waterfront Park. Scanning the menu, we read the description of one beverage in particular. The decadent ingredients: three ounces of Dark Godiva Chocolate, two ounces of White Godiva Chocolate, and one ounce of Chocolate Cream topped with mounds of chocolate shavings sounded incredibly mouthwatering. We all ordered the same hot drink.

"Yum," I exclaimed.

"Wouldn't our patients be astonished to know our dental office's deepest, dark secret is that we are all chocoholics?" I laughed.

Our steaming mugs arrived. Sipping this sumptuous creation, we enjoyed the breathtaking nighttime views of Charleston. It was chilly, but the warmth of our cups and the blazing firepit had us all feeling toasty with a contented glow on our faces.

Feeling energized, we skipped our way back to the Pink Lady. These four senior citizens were as giddy as school girls. I attributed our festive mood to the beautiful memories we'd shared over twenty-five years. Since Ruth was an integral part of the group, we were anxious to return to reminisce. We barged in the door, laughing quite loudly.

With her camera ready, Ruth looked at us in shock as she captured the moment on film. "What happened to you guys on that rooftop?" she questioned.

As I handed Ruth a souvenir menu, I replied, "Nothing, we enjoyed steaming cups of hot chocolate loaded with whipped cream. Can you believe they had a triple serving of Godiva chocolate in them? It was so yummy!"

"Well," I confessed, "We also split a Godiva Truffle Molten Lava Cake with Baileys Irish Cream whipped topping and chocolate sprinkles."

Ruth's puzzlement turned to laughter. She chuckled as she read the description on the menu we brought back. "No wonder the drink was called *One Hot Lady Godiva*."

"Ruth, you should have come with us. Exactly what do you mean...no wonder?" I bubbled. We couldn't control our sidesplitting laughter.

"Oh, my," Ruth couldn't contain herself any longer. "My dear inebriated friends," she continued laughing. "I must inform you that Godiva is a chocolate liqueur, not chocolate syrup. Godiva enhanced your drink monumentally! Ladies, you had at least six ounces of liqueur in that toddy, and there's no telling how much alcohol was in the lava cake."

Swaying back and forth, I murmured, "Mmm…I wondered why those first sips tasted so delightful, unlike any hot chocolate I ever had!"

PART FOUR

Southern Connection

2005-2012

67

Our Crazy Cat Lady

Becky, our receptionist, was known to our dental staff as *Our Crazy Cat Lady*. Three years ago, she purchased a house situated on a ten-acre parcel with a massive wildflower garden. Light, airy grasses complement the colorful display, forming a stunning border that perfumes the air with a sweet lemon scent.

Becky said, "Honestly, I think the cats have an underground network that broadcasts my location. They know I can't turn away a momma cat ready to deliver."

In the time that I have known her, the number of homeless mousers that have appeared on Becky's doorstep was nearing triple digits.

One day our boss noticed several patient charts with green stickers. He was proud of the coding system he initiated. Red was for patients that needed an antibiotic before dental work, yellow was for drug allergies, and blue was for latex allergies.

"Becky, what are these green stickers?" he asked.

Embarrassed, Becky admitted she devised a system of flagging our dental charts to know which patients she could call when another batch of kittens was born.

He laughed, "Good idea. I know none of your co-workers are interested in any more cats. Guess you have to ask other people."

The veterinarian across the parking lot in our office complex kept a running tab in accounts receivable for Becky. She walked through the door bringing in still another sickly-looking cat. Since strays tend to be skittish around people, the veterinarian was amazed that each stray cat looked so comfortable in Becky's arms.

The vet commented, "I think every cat without a roof over its head knows how to get to your house."

"I don't know how to describe it, Doc, but I've observed some aggressive playfulness after the cats roamed my garden. It seemed like they were rolling head-over-tail in kitty bliss."

Becky happened to have a photo of her prized garden, and the veterinarian studied it closely and smiled. It turns out that the previous owners never disclosed the property's uniqueness, which attracted every stray cat in the county. Unbeknownst to Becky, plants that are similar to catnip filled her garden.

"I was always puzzled how you seemed to be the refuge to so many strays. Now I know why!" the vet said with a chuckle. "It's a wonder more cats haven't found their way to your house." He continued to laugh.

The vet tech took the cat from Becky and prepared the feline for the exam. First, the doctor spread the cat's cheeks and lips to reveal red, puffy, bleeding gums filled with pus.

Not giving it another thought, the doctor grabbed a scaler, an instrument used daily in a dental office. He said, "Look, your cat has a severe gum infection."

He proceeded to flick off a piece of debris from the cat's teeth. Becky watched in horror. It became a bloody projectile hurdling through the air, landing on Becky's face. She turned ghastly pale, and Becky's head bounced off the floor when she fainted dead away.

Hoping not to have to call 911, the veterinarian quickly attended to Becky with smelling salts.

"What happened?" He asked when she came around.

Becky's nostrils flared as she tried to suppress her anger. Finally, she managed to say with a shaky voice, "Are you crazy? Why did you do that when I was in the room?"

The veterinarian needed clarification. "Don't you work for the dentist?"

Trying to calm herself, Becky emphatically replied, "Yes, I work for that d-e-n-t-i-s-t! I answer the p-h-o-n-e-s because the sight of blood makes me w-o-o-z-y."

Apologizing profusely, the veterinarian told the pale woman, "This office visit is on the house."

Becky shook her head. "That's great, Doc; you must admit this is a hard way to get a discount. Maybe I should have passed out at an earlier visit."

68

Decoration Day

While living in Tennessee, I noticed more and more how the Southerners respected their deceased loved ones. On Wednesday mornings, the local radio station even had a weekly obituary update so you could plan your week accordingly.

I drove past several cemeteries daily and observed that gravesites were elaborate and beautified with wreaths or flower bouquets. In the North, we called the holiday Memorial Day. Yes, it was a day to honor the deceased military, but it was officially Decoration Day in the South, where all deceased family members are remembered. Since it's a holiday, families reserve time to decorate the graves of loved ones.

My co-worker, Rosemary, clarified and explained Southern cemetery etiquette. It was understood and expected for relatives, even if they had to travel great distances, to be present to honor the family that had passed. Often this resembled a family reunion as kinfolk would gather to pay tribute to their deceased. Frequently, a potluck dinner would follow.

Rosemary explained it was especially important for the family to travel eighty miles to "decorate" her grandfather's final resting place this year. She continued that the family was still reeling from the unforgettable catastrophe at the funeral. Everyone needed the time to heal.

The grandfather's funeral procession took place last autumn as the leaves were brilliantly peaking to perfection. The service was held locally, and the burial would occur in a private ceremony on the mountain the next day.

Solemnly, pallbearers carried Grandpa's casket up the steep church steps. Ascending the fifteen stairs to the vestibule, they found keeping the casket level impossible. The pallbearers felt the weight shift in the casket, and all at once, without warning, the bottom fell out of the coffin. The horrified family witnessed Grandpa bouncing head over heels down the church steps.

Aunt Emmy screamed and fainted while others shrieked. There wasn't anything one could do to calm the crowd. Finally, the distressed minister ushered the mourners inside the church while the panicked funeral director quickly retrieved the body and damaged casket.

Upon returning to the funeral home, the mortician found his partner had failed to mention he'd purchased the casket from a new distributor. Upon further investigation, they realized this particular casket model was very economical because it had a weight limit. Grandpa's cumbersome body was too much for the flimsy construction.

Weary mourners waited inside, praying. Many were distraught and inconsolable. The organist tried to soothe the mourners by playing familiar hymns. Nothing could placate the relatives. The funeral would have to take place another day.

A few weeks after the funeral fiasco, it was time to bury Grandpa. Loving the rugged character of the Blue Ridge Mountains, Grandpa had purchased ten acres of pristine mountain property on a lower elevation of its highest peak years before twenty-six- hundred acres of the picturesque mountain became a state park.

An early winter storm approached. As wispy snowflakes fell, coating the eyelashes of the mourners and mixing with their tears, Grandpa was peacefully laid in his final resting place. He found his little bit of heaven on earth. Grandpa's burial plot is, ironically, near the base of Grandfather Mountain.

69

Am I Gone?

I had recently moved from Rochester, NY, to Tennessee, and it took me a while to acclimate to living in the South. However, after paying my respects during calling hours for a co-worker's grandfather at Newcomers Funeral Parlor, I noticed several local mortuaries were very awkwardly named.

Often undertakers use the family surname, which, in theory, would be a good idea unless the name gives way to mortuaries called Butcher's Funeral Home, Cooks & Burns Crematory, and last but not to be forgotten, Baloney's Funeral Chapel. Wondering what these proprietors were thinking, I cracked a smile, rationalizing it was probably weird mortician humor.

I realized such funeral home names were not exclusive to the South. A mortuary back home featured on national news and the *Ellen Degeneres Show* also had a satirical name. Boasting fifteen convenient locations in Western New York, this business carried the family name Amigone (AM I GONE).

A few weeks after her Grandpa's burial, Rosemary showed me the back window of her SUV. Covering the entire rear windshield was a memorial sticker with huge letters recording the grandfather's name, year of birth, and death, boasting beloved husband, father, and grandfather. I had never seen these displays on vehicles until I moved to the South.

The next day I was driving behind a truck. Covering the entire rear window was a commemorative message that caught my attention. It read, "Cruising for my Son, in Loving Memory of Henry, June 1975-August 2012.

I thought *how sad he died at such a young age. That was just a few months ago.* However, the sentiment underneath his name is what stunned me. In bold-faced letters, "Beer Sucker" was written under the date. I chuckled and wondered if that was what caused his demise.

Still laughing, I pulled into my destination, parking next to a huge black car. As I walked past the vehicle, I noticed it had a front license plate that made me do a double-take. Pictured on the plate was a photograph of a distinguished-looking woman with a cross on either side of her picture. Above the striking woman's photo, written in dark-blue lettering, it simply said "Thelma R.I.P." Ironically, in the next parking space, "Bury It" was the message on the vanity plate.

What a strange series of events, I thought. Not wanting to be irreverent, I shook my head to stifle my laughter. It was just too much of a coincidence. Not to be disrespectful, but my mind went to the thought, "I wonder what Thelma would think of the Beer Sucker?'"

70

Speedway at the Biltmore Estate

Most people don't realize there is a hidden pathway through the gardens at the Biltmore Estate in Asheville, NC. After our discovery, Connie and I affectionately coined the path, the *Biltmore Speedway.*

Our dental office was on a team-building adventure at The Biltmore Mansion. The tour had inaccessible areas for Connie on her motorized scooter, so we split off from the group. We chatted as I walked alongside Connie. Oblivious to anything other than the tranquility we were feeling, we failed to notice the paved path had turned into a narrow gravel trail.

Realizing that we had probably strayed too far, I asked Connie, "Are you ready to turn around? We left our jackets in the van; the skies look dark and stormy."

The scooter stopped abruptly, and Connie said, "Uh, Ohhhh!"

It was indeed a sentiment I didn't want to hear. Seeing the panicked expression on Connie's face, I asked, "What's the matter?"

In a shaky voice, Connie said, "My scooter won't turn on; the gauge indicates low battery power."

With a worried expression, I said, "Connie, I know I'll never be able to push you back on that scooter. That ramp we took had quite a slope to it."

Connie's eyes filled with tears. "You'll have to go for help alone. I'll be okay."

I hated to leave, but the journey back to the mansion was much shorter since I could take the traditional route and not follow the winding ramp. Huffing and puffing, I climbed the last flight of stairs, and the mansion was in sight. Exhausted, I flagged down a security guard. He was resting, perched on a ledge, not very interested in what I had to say.

Explaining our plight, I asked, "Do you have a golf cart or an ATV?"

He looked at me with a puzzled expression and said, "No, ma'am, we don't."

Waiting for him to offer assistance, I pleaded that we needed help. He smirked and commented, "You know, I saw you two going down that hill and thought, I hope they have a good charge on that thing."

Annoyed and impatient, I replied, "Please, can you at least call for help on that walkie-talkie?"

Blankly, he stared at me. I was ready to grab the hand radio when he finally reacted. He summoned one of the maintenance crew. Our rescue mission began as we retraced my steps.

It seemed like an eternity, but we found Connie. Imagine that, just where I left her.

"Connie, I'm so sorry it took so long."

The man asked, "Can you walk?" As the man watched Connie shake her head, he assessed our predicament. "Can you disengage the gears?"

Connie was worried as she replied, "Yes, but that means I have no brakes and little control of the steering."

I watched him ponder over the information. "Well, even with two of us pushing, I don't think we'll get you up that hill. However, there is a service road not far from here. We could try it, but it's all downhill."

"I guess we have no other alternative," I commented. "Connie, we'll try to hang on to keep you safe."

We started along the steep path, and Connie's scooter began gaining speed. We jogged along, but the pace became too fast. I watched in horror as the scooter careened nearly out of control.

Terrified, I could hardly hear Connie's screams over my own. There was no way to slow her down. Connie was precariously close to the path's edge with a sheer drop on either side. Somehow, miraculously, her instinct kicked in. Connie leaned into the turns, giving her some stability. Zigzagging down the road with expert precision, she looked like she did this every day. Connie navigated the curves until the scooter lost momentum, and she was safe.

As we caught up, I breathed a heavy sigh of relief. "Connie, you looked incredible, like a motorcycle stunt driver."

The shuttle driver explained the handicapped van had a malfunctioning ramp, so I had no other option but to leave Connie alone again to retrieve her lift-equipped vehicle. A slight drizzle started to fall, with storm clouds rapidly approaching. This beautiful outing had become a disaster, one complicated element at a time.

Returning with the van, I approached Connie again in the same spot I had left her. As luck would have it, when Connie turned the key, one burst of power was left in the scooter. Connie had safely transferred to the van, and the scooter was on the lift when the skies opened up in a downpour.

Something caught my eye just as we met up with our group from the office. I burst out laughing, "Connie, why is it every time we go somewhere, it turns into an episode from *I Love Lucy*? Look at your scooter."

Now, everyone joined in the laughter. On the front of the scooter was the license plate I had given Connie years ago. It was a picture of Lucille Ball with a mock vanity plate reading "SPEED IT UP."

As we all continued to giggle, I turned to Connie and said, "I guess I'm going to have to find one that reads *SLOW IT DOWN*."

71

Implant Debacle

Implant dentistry has been around for several years. However, recent breakthroughs in technique and technology now provide opportunities for dentists in general practice, not only specialists, to perform implants.

Working in our office was a recent high school graduate enrolled in the local college's dental assistant program. Young and energetic, Marcie was eager to learn. Dr. Webster, our employer, had begun placing dental implants, and Marcie was fascinated.

Earlier that day, I checked the schedule and noticed Sinclair, a favorite patient of mine, was coming in for his regular appointment. Sinclair speaks in a heavy German accent and is sometimes difficult to understand.

Over the past six years, we have had many meaningful conversations and have built a strong patient-hygienist relationship. I knew he had undergone surgery last year and complimented how well he looked.

I noticed that Sinclair's health history needed updating. It's of utmost importance that the dentist is aware of any medical condition or medication that could affect treatment. Medical history forms are necessary but often confusing, and patients resent constantly revising the information.

Some forms are like a mini pop quiz. This particular document had the question: "What is Periodontal Disease?" Most people left it blank. The originators of the questionnaire should have put it in layman's terms, asking, "What is gum disease?"

Glancing at the completed sheet, I giggled at the most creative and imaginative answer I had ever seen. Having a great sense of humor, Sinclair responded to the question: "Periodontals are giant dinosaurs that roamed the earth millions of years ago."

Thinking Marcie would be amused, I gave her the opportunity to review his comical answer with him. After instructing her to update Sinclair's medical paperwork, I left the room. Marcie was so intent on getting everything correct that she got carried away when she saw "implant" checked on the health form and never even saw the hilarious answer about dinosaurs.

She grabbed a mouth mirror and was obsessed with determining which tooth was the implant. She couldn't figure it out. Still, Marcie was confused because, typically, an implant would have a crown visible in the mouth. Finally, Marcie said quite loudly, "Dr. Webster did a magnificent job since I can't distinguish the correct tooth." Exasperated, she finally asked Sinclair, "Where is the implant?"

Marcie looked impatient, and Sinclair looked stunned. Turning very pale, he hesitated. Then, insistently, Marcie inquired again, "I can't find the implant. Can you show me?"

I was within earshot of the treatment room when I heard the conversation, but I was too late to intervene. Sinclair took a minute to compose himself. He tried to find the correct words in English but he wasn't sure he could explain so, slowly, in a shy, embarrassed move; Sinclair looked down and pointed to his privates, where he had a different, more personal type of implant.

Marcie let out an audible gasp, turned beet red, and bolted from the treatment room. I ran into the room. "Sinclair, I had no idea Marcie would embarrass you. I'm so sorry."

Sinclair was understanding and a good sport. But, on the other hand, Marcie was so upset that she was sent home for the afternoon.

Dr. Webster came into the treatment room to provide damage control and said, "Sinclair, now I guess we'll have to find a spot to do a dental implant."

Thankfully, they were past the awkward situation and had a hardy laugh.

72

Wild Kingdom Bunco

As a Northerner, I was beginning to experience a totally different way of life in Dixie. A lovely lady named Pearl was one of my first patients in a Southern dental office. She was in her eighties but had more spunk and vigor than most people half her age. I introduced myself in my unmistakable Western New York accent.

Pearl immediately commented, "You ain't from around here, honey."

Shrugging in agreement, I realized I needed to learn the Southern ways. It always made me smile to hear everyone, including doctors, call you honey or sweetie.

Pearl was a proper Southern Belle. There is no mistaking it, good manners matter in the South, and Pearl wanted to make me feel welcome by extending her friendship.

As we chatted, she told me it was her night to host Bunco. "I want to learn that game," I confessed.

Pearl invited me to join her substitute list. About a week later, Pearl called, "My group is shy of two players tonight, and I wondered if you were free and could bring a friend."

Pearl explained a new member, Robin, was hosting for the first time and gave me the address. I invited Mary, a fellow

Yankee, thinking this opportunity seemed perfect for us to meet more people.

We arrived at the designated time. As the hostess opened her front door, we faced two huge, snarling Rottweilers. Mary and I looked at each other, but she assured us the dogs were gentle. Pleased to find they left us alone, we began to mingle.

Looking around the room, we noticed an extensive collection of photographs. Mary and I were trying to determine what these unrecognizable images were.

Robin gushed, "Oh, you're looking at pictures of my babies." They didn't resemble any baby we had ever seen, so I refrained from commenting.

Soon the group assembled, and we were ready to play. As the bell rang to start the game, I noticed Mary's face became ashen. She stared with her eyes practically bugging out of her head.

Turning to look, I soon realized why she was panicked. Two enormous possums were entering the room. *Doesn't anyone else see these animals?* I thought.

One possum proceeded to leap onto the furniture and crawled across the kitchen counter; the other possum moseyed under the tables while we played.

Assuming I would be safe, I made my way to the restroom. But, boy, was I wrong! To my horror, I encountered a possum using a litter box. Before it could pounce on me, I dashed out of there faster than any possum could possibly scurry. Indeed, I'd had enough!

It was time to get out of there! I gave Mary a frantic eye roll and told our hostess that I was getting a migraine. We left in a hurry, well before the evening was officially over. As we made our hasty exit, we noticed movement on the staircase and watched as a raccoon and two weasels came scampering down the steps. We were leaving just in the nick of time!

Racing to the car, we slammed the doors shut. We weren't taking any chances of animals following us. Mary was unable to conceal her anger. She shook and glared at me, screaming, "You set me up! You set me up! How could you?"

Wracked with laughter, I couldn't even start the car. Mary's anger dissipated, and we fed off each other. We couldn't control ourselves. Crying, laughing, howling, and trying to catch my breath, I assured Mary that I had no idea that we would be playing "Wild Kingdom Bunco."

It dawned on Mary, "Oh my goodness, those photos were of her newborn baby possums."

While still giggling, I commented, "No wonder we couldn't tell what they were."

My friend, who invited us to the Bunco game, called me later that evening. "Bless your little hearts for coming tonight. I had no idea that all those critters inside the house would surround us."

I apologized to her for leaving abruptly, "I just couldn't stand the possum brushing up against my legs. Your friends all have great poker faces."

With a chuckle, Pearl said, "What gets me is that our hostess couldn't understand why no one touched the food she set out on the counter."

Mary laughed when I called her. But then, sarcastically, she added, "Playing possum has taken on a whole new meaning."

73

Smokin' Hot

Isabelle came in for her dental appointment carrying a photograph from last weekend's party sponsored by the couple's club of her church. This particular event was named *A Night to Remember*.

Isabelle laughed, describing the evening, "It was a senior prom, a very, very senior prom with the average participant's age being seventy years young. Men wore tuxedoes while the women sparkled in their ball gowns and jewels."

I oooh-ed and ahh-ed over the photo. "Isabelle, you two look wonderful! Wasn't your husband Robert your date for your high school senior prom? Not many couples can boast they attended the high school senior prom and the geriatric prom fifty years later with the same man."

"That's so true. Isn't that a hoot?" Isabelle exclaimed. "It was a delightful evening that got off to a bad start. Before the party was in full swing, an event that could have been disastrous threatened to ruin our fun."

I was all ears.

Isabelle continued, "Not long after the crowd arrived at the church social hall, heavy smoke poured from the kitchen. A grease fire in the oven caused the smoke detectors to start screeching. Hurriedly, men grabbed fire extinguishers.

After that, things were under control very quickly, or so they thought."

Laughing, she added, "Unbeknownst to us, the smoke alarms were directly linked to the fire department, which sent emergency personnel to the scene. Sirens wailed in the distance as a police car, fire trucks, and EMTs rushed our location. It was utter chaos!"

Robert met the Fire Chief at the door, explaining what had happened. After thoroughly checking the kitchen, the Fire Chief was satisfied there was no longer danger or threat of flames re-igniting. The scene was declared safe, giving the emergency personnel an all-clear signal to leave. Soon, the prom resumed. The anxious crowd returned to the festivities with enthusiasm.

Isabelle chuckled, adding, "The crowd happily returned to the dance floor. Everyone laughed at the choice of songs selected by the delightful DJ as *Smoke Gets in Your Eyes* played over the sound system."

The Fire Chief continued chatting with Robert as he watched the elegant couples twirl around the dance floor gracefully. He was impressed.

"Is this a wedding?" he asked.

Robert stifled a laugh as he said, "No, Chief. I'm afraid this is our version of, umm...our *senior prom.*"

They had a good laugh. The Chief turned to Robert as he headed to the door. "You may be the Medicare crowd, but you sure are a bunch of *smokin' hot seniors.*"

74

An Innocent Gardner

I have special love and connections to our senior citizen patients. Stanley was the last of my dental patients scheduled on a day that had exhausted me. Today, I found it difficult to be cheery and chipper, but I greeted him with a smile.

He was a nice older man, but awkward to position correctly for easy access to his teeth. My back was always killing me after his dental visit, and I had to keep my hands in his mouth to prevent his constant chatter.

Being a generation apart, we had little in common besides the fact we both had moved from Buffalo, NY, to Tennessee. He constantly rehashed stories from yesteryear. Today, another of Stanley's acquaintances was the subject of his latest tale: "Hey, I've got a great story for you. This one's a hoot."

Trying to distract him and still be polite, I told him: "Stanley, I really need to get your teeth cleaned." Unfortunately, I knew from experience that Stanley was not stopping once he was on a roll. I kept my fingers crossed and hoped this would be short.

Stanley didn't even stop for a breath and started rambling: "One day, my buddy Joe found some seeds wrapped in a napkin. When he got home, he planted them, placing the pots in his front window. The plants thrived in the bright sunlit space."

Stanley continued: "Joe was amazed that plants seemed to double in size overnight. In a few weeks, they were almost touching the ceiling. Joe still had no idea what kind of plants he was nurturing."

My mind wandered, conjuring up the image of Jack and the Beanstalk. It made me smile, which helped me hide my annoyance that I couldn't start Stanley's cleaning.

I didn't know where this story was going. I just wanted to do my job and go home. I wasn't at all interested in an umpteenth account of the old neighborhood.

Stanley continued to babble: "One day, at his job, Joe noticed a co-worker's T-shirt with a screen-print picture of the same leaf as the mystery houseplants. Being a friendly sort of guy, Joe pointed to the image and said. 'Hey, those look just like my plants that are growing like weeds. I have to get rid of them before they take over the house.'"

Laughing, Stanley continued: "The young man eagerly offered to take them off Joe's hands. Joe, the innocent gardener, was pleased to share and gave the co-worker the fruits of his labor. Later that week, Joe saw a picture of the same plant in a magazine article. He gasped when he realized that his bumper crop was unmistakably marijuana."

I have to admit, I laughed.

Stanley said. "This happened years ago, but maybe you know him."

He was always trying to connect me to the old neighborhood and thought I should know everyone who ever lived in Buffalo. I tried to look interested, but it was rare that I knew any of his neighbors.

Stanley insisted there might be some recognition. "Maybe you know him by his unique nickname. It's Piap."

I shook my head in disbelief. I couldn't suppress a chuckle that burst into hearty laughter as I thought *this story was priceless! Why had I not heard about this before?*

When I finally was able to compose myself, I was able to say: "Yes, Stanley, I do know him very, very well. You see, Stanley, Piap is my father's nickname. I guess it's a good thing I didn't have to post bail for him."

75

A Southern Belle's Exhumation

Weeks after her brother's funeral, Rowena came for her dental appointment. I expressed my sympathy and settled into my regular routine of taking blood pressure and updating her medical history. I commented that her blood pressure was running high.

She replied, "No wonder after the series of events that happened at the funeral!" Since most people don't refer to a funeral as a series of events, I anxiously awaited an explanation. Rowena's comment definitely piqued my interest.

Always impeccably dressed and coiffed, Rowena is the epitome of the true Southern Belle. A perfectionist, always meticulously paying attention to detail, her brother's funeral would be no different. As is very typical in East Tennessee, the family plot is on the side of a mountain. Wanting the gravesite to be perfect, she decided to make sure everything was in order. She chose to visit the private cemetery in the morning, just before the funeral.

Heavy rains had made the red clay very slippery. Already dressed for church, Rowena was glad to find that she didn't sink into the mud. However, as she approached the grave, she found that her dress shoes had no traction.

Much to her dismay, her feet went out from under her. She slid on the wet ground landing on her derriere. Unable to stop, she continued to slide until she tumbled into the open grave. *Thwack!* The sound was so loud that it could be heard for miles. She gasped! She was too stunned to scream.

She told me that a quick overview revealed she had only hit her head and skinned her knees. "But not to worry," she murmured to herself. "I'm a limber sixty-five-year-old, and I'll shimmy myself out of this hole with no problem." She continued, "I felt I could just put my elbows on the side of the grave and pull myself up."

Attempting to rescue herself proved to be an impossible task. The side walls were incredibly slick. Rowena realized that six feet was a long, long way down. "How am I ever going to get out?" she whimpered.

She tried to hold back the tears, but they poured down her cheeks. Rowena looked at her mud-caked watch. Sheer panic gripped her. She thought, "Everyone will wonder where I am. What will happen if I am in the grave when they bring the casket?" Her imagination was running wild, but this was a definite possibility.

In lonely desperation, she started jumping up and down with her hands frantically waving in the air. She continued to jump and jump, trying to grasp anything with her fingertips. Exasperated, Rowena was exhausted and giving up hope.

It just so happens the Cooley Brothers were heading to their favorite hunting spot up English Mountain. The road had multiple switchbacks, so traveling had to be at a reasonable speed. Gazing out the window, daydreaming, Jimmy Bob saw something out of the corner of his eye. He turned to his brother and said, "I know you are going to think I am crazy, but I think I saw a hand coming out of that grave." Jasper dismissed it, chuckling, "Jimmy Bob, I think you hit the moonshine a little early today."

They continued to drive up the mountain.

Jimmy Bob couldn't shake that nagging feeling that what he saw was real. Out of curiosity and to prove a point, he convinced his brother to turn around. Sure enough, there was movement. As they exited the car and approached the grave, fingertips were visible. Peering down, they were astonished. They saw a mud-covered woman in a frenzied hysteria with arms flailing. Rowena was a sorry sight.

Jimmy Bob and Jasper returned to the truck for a heavy-duty rope and lowered it into the hole. Rowena tied it around her waist. Then, using their brute strength, the brothers managed to "exhume" Rowena from her brother's final resting place. The entire time, the Cooley Brothers never said a word. Silently they pulled her out. Then they left without asking so much as "Are you alright?"

Rowena knelt in the mud, trembling. After cautiously getting away from the side of the grave, she continued to slip and stumble as she made her way to the car. Shocked to see the time, Rowena shrieked, "I am going to be late for the funeral. I need to rush home to clean up. Oh…my… gosh! I have to hurry!"

Unbelievably, she was able to compose herself and change her clothing. She drove to the church and attended the beautiful church service. When the mourners arrived at the cemetery, Rowena's daughter, Gracie, noticed her mother's bruises.

As the preacher prayed aloud, Rowena whispered the story to her daughter. Horrified, Gracie admonished her mother and started wailing, which is perfectly acceptable at a funeral. Still stunned, Gracie continued to blubber. She couldn't erase that dramatic image flashing through her mind. Soon, the vivid mental picture of her mother wallowing in the muddy hole turned her sobs into uncontrollable laughter.

Gracie and Rowena hung their heads. Then, contritely, they lowered their eyes. Automatically, each woman covered her mouth with both hands but failed miserably at concealing their chortling. Flabbergasted, the preacher looked up and clenched his jaw. Sighing heavily, he continued to pray louder while the annoyed mourners turned to them and scowled.

Rowena continued to tell me the rest of the story. By this time, the entire dental office staff had gathered around my treatment room. Naturally, everyone was curious to see what was causing all the boisterous laughter. Rowena and I could no longer contain ourselves. We were howling. Tears streamed down our cheeks. Now, she had to tell the story all over again, causing us to practically hyperventilate.

I turned to Rowena, trying to apologize to her. "It was really insensitive of me to laugh so hard." I tried to say with a straight face. "I am so sorry for your loss, but that is the funniest story I have ever heard!"

About the Author

Terry Hans grew up in Buffalo, New York, and attended Erie County Technical Institute's dental hygiene program. She completed her studies, took the state and national licensing exams, and became a Registered Dental Hygienist (RDH). It was there Terry found her calling. She realized most people were nervous and fearful of dental treatment, so she began using humor to relax her patients.

She married Butch after college and had two daughters, Tracey and Christy. Terry became inspired to write when her first grandson was due to arrive. She composed poems and created scrapbooks to capture his childhood. Along came three more grandsons prompting Terry to continue developing her writing skills.

After working in Buffalo for ten years, Terry and her family moved to Rochester, New York. She worked part-time in separate offices for two fabulous dentists. Working for one employer for twenty-five years and the other fourteen years, Terry built strong relationships with patients and staff; most of her stories are from this time.

In 2005, Terry and her husband moved to the South. Terry began to hone her writing skills by attending classes and workshops, and sharing ideas with published writers.

Terry continued to search for ways to improve her writing skills. When the couple moved to North Carolina in 2012,

Terry was blessed to be invited to join two established writing groups, NC Scribes and Light of Carolina Christians Writers. It was here an idea for a book materialized.

With the assistance of these award-winning authors, this compilation of stories came to life. She writes about experiences her patients have shared and reveals comical occurrences that transpired while working in dental offices.

Terry has been published multiple times in *Chicken Soup for the Soul* collections. She contributed stories and poems to the award-winning anthology *9/11-That Beautiful Broken Day*. She is excited to publish her first book, *Laugh, Rinse, Repeat*.

Printed in Great Britain
by Amazon

32182516R00154